Farewell to the Family?

Public Policy and Family Breakdown In Britain and the USA

Patricia Morgan

IEA Health and Welfare Unit
London, 1995

First published January 1995

The IEA Health and Welfare Unit
2 Lord North St
London SW1P 3LB

© The IEA Health and Welfare Unit 1995

ISBN 0-255 36356-7

Front cover clipart supplied by
Image Club Graphics Inc
for Corel Draw 5

Typeset by the IEA Health and Welfare Unit
in New Century Schoolbook 10 on 11 point
Printed in Great Britain by
Goron Pro-Print Co. Ltd
Churchill Industrial Estate, Lancing, West Sussex

Contents

	Page
Foreword	
David G. Green	iv
The Author	v
Introduction	1
The Breaking of the Modern Family	3
Perpetuating Poverty	27
Money and Marriage	50
By Chance or Design?	82
Same Incomes, Same Outcomes?	113
Conclusion	152
Tables	156
Figures	161
Appendix	164
Notes	166

Foreword

H AS BRITAIN been conducting an unwitting experiment in the abolition of the family? In *Farewell to the Family?* Patricia Morgan shows how, step by step, the traditional family of man, wife and children is being replaced by the mother-child-state unit. She warns that this development is doubly harmful. First, the children of broken families tend to suffer: they under-perform at school, grow physically less well, experience more illness, and are more likely to turn to crime and drugs. And second, young men who ought to be assuming the responsibilities of fatherhood, adopt instead an unattached and predatory lifestyle which often brings them into conflict with the police.

As the endnotes testify, *Farewell to the Family?* is based on an exhaustive survey of the evidence and Patricia Morgan deserves high praise for her efforts. Her book is a worthy successor to the earlier books in this series, such as *Families Without Fatherhood* in which Norman Dennis and A.H. Halsey first called the attention of the political left to family breakdown, *The Family: Is It Just Another Lifestyle Choice?*, in which Brigitte Berger and others drew attention to the neglected merits of the traditional family, and *The Emerging British Underclass*, in which Charles Murray urged Britons not to repeat mistakes already made in his American homeland.

David G. Green

The Author

Patricia Morgan, Senior Research Fellow in the family at the IEA's Health and Welfare Unit, is a sociologist specialising in criminology and family policy. She is the author or co-author of a number of books including: *Delinquent Phantasies*, 1978; *Facing Up to Family Income*, 1989; *The Hidden Costs of Childcare*, 1992; and *Families in Dreamland*, 1992. She has contributed chapters to *Full Circle, Family Portraits,* and *The Loss of Virtue*, as well as articles for periodicals and national newspapers. Patricia Morgan is a frequent contributor to television and radio programmes and is presently writing a full-length work on the relationship between capitalism and the family.

I know of no single instance in anthropological literature of a community where illegitimate children, that is children of unmarried girls, would enjoy the same social treatment and have the same social status as legitimate ones. The universal postulate of legitimacy has a great sociological significance ... It means that in all human societies moral tradition and the law decree that the group consisting of a woman and her offspring is not a socially complete unit. The ruling of culture runs here ... it declares that the human family must consist of a male as well as a female.

Bronislaw Malinowski,
Sex and Repression in Savage Society, 1927.

The only real family is the mother and her baby. Everyone else is peripheral.

Claire Rayner,
The Jewish Chronicle, 17 June 1994.

Introduction

D ISCUSSION of family affairs is heavily focused on lone parents, and a plethora of reports now dwell upon their disadvantaged position and how this might be addressed. Indeed, the lone parent is now the reference point in discussions of child poverty, and provides the context for more general considerations of child-rearing costs. Lone parents are represented as caught in the poverty and unemployment traps of the means-tested benefits system as if they alone are affected. Clearly, not only are they felt to constitute the poor in the non-aged population, as well as the carers and the family providers—*they are the families for whom 'family policy' is designed*. Married couples with children have dropped below the eyeline of public policy-makers

Once when a 'family wage' was mentioned it referred to the various ways in which the living standards of the married-couple household were sustained, as husband and wife covered the tasks of childrearing through mutual support. Now, not only are there 'packages' for lone parents—supplements and substitutes that will enable all aspects of the parental role to be invested in one person—but the predicament of the mother and child unit dominates public policy debate. Support and care do not have recognition when they occur in the context of the two-parent family. This is accompanied by the imperative to put more of childraising into the public domain—not least to ensure the viability of all 'family forms' or conditions in which mothers have children.

These changes might seem to occur piecemeal, but they are also the outcome of a concerted effort to ensure that the married family is no longer recognised in law nor supported economically. Undeclared, this objective has been systematically pursued with no understanding of the consequences for society, and without public debate. Since the 1970s, a climate of hostility to the family has provided the general context in which its legal and economic foundations have been easily undermined. Not least, it has given politicians undefended spoils for the taking, with which to replenish the public coffers, distribute favours and buy off shrill sectional interests. But, more particularly, those of an anti-family or feminist orientation have increasingly come to dominate that part of the academic culture dealing with

1

marriage, divorce, family benefits and taxation. They occupy the key positions on research bodies, committees and charities concerned with children. They have their own pressure groups financed from Brussels and Westminster, issue directives from Europe and, in the 1990s, sit at the right hand of government ministers directing the demolition process.

This book begins by examining what the increase in lone parents represents in demographic terms; their economic status and treatment by the tax-benefit system compared to families; and how provisions for this group have developed. It goes on to look at the idea that there has been a 'feminisation of poverty', under which lone mothers have come to represent the poorest of the poor. After looking at the nature and origins of present-day poverty, the discussion turns to the causes of lone parenthood itself. It is suggested that this lies in the impoverishment of the two-parent family, which, instead of receiving consideration or protection in the face of adverse labour market developments, has faced an increased tax burden, as virtually all the support families once enjoyed has been withdrawn with increasing speed.

With policies based on the mother-child unit and with men facing strong disincentives to assume the father role, we may expect fewer two-parent families to form. If we ask what are the relative costs of making the mother-child unit the pre-eminent childrearing form, these include not only the financial provisions necessary for its direct support, but those to ensure that it is 'fully functional' in terms of outcomes that are on a par, or compare favourably, with those of two-parent families. Thus, we must look at areas from mortality to crime to see if it is feasible, let alone possible, for public services to fill the gaps left by the dissolution and disappearance of two-parent families. We also have to ask if these measures could ever tackle the changes to the social structure itself, with all the implications for social order and economic productivity, represented by the disengagement of men from family life.

The Breaking of the Modern Family

Summary: There has been a rapid increase in the formation of lone-parent families. Births out of wedlock now constitute a large percentage of all births, but the apparently exponential rise has much to do with the collapse of the married birth rate, which means that out-of-wedlock births constitute an ever-growing percentage of all births. The majority of lone parents depend upon public assistance, and as a result are spoken of as if they constitute the poorest families. However, couples with children outnumber lone-parent families in the lowest income groups. Despite claims that the tax and benefit systems discriminate against lone parents, the lone parent receives more at every level of earnings than the married couple with children. The burden of taxation has increasingly been shifted onto married parents to the benefit of the single and the childless. The traditional concept of the family wage has been abandoned together with the recognition that taxation should be related to the number of dependants on an income. An elaborate means-tested and selective benefits system has taken its place which is now being developed as something almost exclusively for lone parents.

From broken marriages to no marriages

BETWEEN 1971 and 1991 the number of lone-parent households more than doubled (from 570,000 to 1,300,000) as did the number of children living in those households (from one million to 2.2 million). As a percentage of the whole population, those living in such households increased by four times (see Table 1.1, p. 156). Britain's proportion of lone-parent families (one in five of all families with dependent children) is catching up with America's one in four.[1] Up to 1984 nearly three-quarters of the increase was attributable to the rise in divorced and separated mothers, as the number of children under 16 involved in divorce grew steadily from 145,000 in 1975 to 161,000 in 1991. As rates of remarriage have fallen over the past couple of decades, this has reinforced the impact of rising divorce on the number of lone-parents (see Table 1.2, p. 156).

But lone parenthood is increasingly the result of a huge growth in never-married mothers. In 1971 they were the smallest group; by 1991, they were the largest (see Table 1.3, p. 157). Births outside marriage went into vertical ascent in the 1980s, as the one baby in ten born to an unmarried mother in the late 1970s rose to over three in ten in the early 1990s, with the rate (at 31 per cent in 1992) now rising by around two percentage points a year. Among those births occurring to women under 20 it is 84 per cent. However, the rise in all age-groups is illustrated by the way in which a fifth of all births to women over 35 are now outside marriage, compared with a tenth in 1982.

While almost three-quarters of these births are registered by both parents, and are often officially characterised as occurring within stable relationships, this leaves a substantial minority occurring to mothers of undisputed single status.[2] Moreover, less than three-quarters of the joint registrations involve the same address. Data from the 1988 and 1989 General Household Survey showed that 7 out of 10 never-married mothers were living *without* a stable partner.

Informal relationships also break up at a far higher rate than marriages and the instability is growing. From the 1981 Census it was possible to estimate that 60 per cent of jointly-registered children under 10 born to unmarried parents were still living with two parents, compared to 90 per cent of children with married parents.[3] One small-scale study showed how nearly half the women cohabiting at the time of conception were alone by the time the child was aged 21 months. Nearly all the women who were married were *not* lone mothers by the same time.[4] The same trends started earlier in the USA but the pace of change has been faster in the UK.

Births outside marriage may reflect either, or both, changes in the unwed birthrate relative to the marital birthrate, or changes in the proportion of women of childbearing age who are unmarried and therefore 'at risk' of having births outside marriage.

A convenient way of looking at these movements is to calculate the number of children a woman is likely to have over her lifetime while she is single by asking what would have happened if the birthrate for that year had applied throughout the woman's lifetime. In America in 1960 a typical white woman could expect to have 0.08 illegitimate births over her lifetime and, in 1987, to have 0.29. This is not a large absolute increase but a big percentage increase. Among blacks the increase was from 1.05 to 1.43, a larger absolute increase but a smaller percentage increase than among whites. By themselves these figures do not suggest a massive rise in illegitimacy. However, in 1960 both white and black *married* women in the USA could expect to have 3.5 children. By 1987 a white married woman could expect only 1.81 and a black married woman 0.81. It is this precipitous decline in births to married women that helps to make the unwed birthrate assume great proportions.

Similar trends are obvious in the UK. With falling marriage rates, births to unmarried women represent an increasing proportion of the total. In 1971 80 per cent of women were married by the age of 25, but in 1990 half were single. Not surprisingly, the growth in single women and fatherless children is accompanied by a steep decline in the male marriage rate. Over the last two decades the number of males who had never been married by the age of 29 has grown from 26 per cent to half.

To this one must add the declining fertility of married women compared to that of single women. The average age at first birth is higher than at any time since modern records began, at 26.0 for all women and 27.8 years for married women. The average family size grew for every kind of lone mother between 1981-91 as that of married couples continued to fall (see Table 1.4, p. 158). The contribution of extra-marital fertility to total fertility more than doubled over the 1980s (see Figure 1, p. 161). Thus the decrease in the overall birthrate since the mid-1970s overwhelmingly represents the decline in births to married women. Fewer married women are having second or subsequent births and more are having no children at all.

It is important to set the larger family size and earlier family building of lone mothers in the context of the way that the birthrate has been well below replacement for an unparalleled length of time. In order for a population to replace itself a woman must have an average of 2.1 children over the course of her childbearing years, but fertility fell below this level in Britain in the early part of the 1970s and shows no sign of any sharp upward turn (see Figure 1, p. 161). There is a steadily rising proportion of women who have never had children. Amongst those born in 1945, 11 per cent were childless at age 35, but this proportion had almost doubled for women born ten years later.[5] This contributes to the way in which the type of household that is increasing most rapidly contains neither a married couple nor a lone parent, but one single, childless person. Nearly one in ten households by the end of the century will comprise a man under pensionable age living alone.[6] The population must either decline or be augmented, as it has been, by immigration and the extension of the life expectancy of the very old.

Sources of income

The proportion of lone parents in employment dropped in the 1980s, at a time when that of working married mothers was on the rise. By the 1990s the proportion of lone mothers with a child under 5 in employment was almost half that of married mothers.[7]

Instead, around 7 out of 10 lone parents came to obtain all or much of their income from public assistance. By 1986, 93 per cent of never-married mothers derived their incomes in this way. The lone-parent population is not, of course, made up of the same people over time. What the figures represent are the larger numbers forming the lone-parent population in the 1980s, who were likely to go on basic benefit, compared to their counterparts in the 1970s. Income Support is payable to lone parents without having to seek work until children are 16, and the proportion depending on it rose from 37 per cent to over two-thirds between 1971 and 1989. According to one study, 85 per cent of women who had been lone parents had been in receipt of Income Support at some stage.[8] In contrast, only 12.5 per cent of families headed by a couple was dependent on Income Support in 1987, and earnings were the main source of income for 86 per cent.[9] A snapshot of 33-year-old parents provided by a longitudinal study in 1991 showed how 58 per cent of the income of lone mothers came from public assistance—as against 14 per cent for couples with children—and 43 per cent relied totally on benefits.[10] Single people are, anyway, more likely to receive their income from the state and non-labour sources than the married; single men have higher rates of unemployment or economic inactivity than their married counterparts.

Dependence upon Income Support also became a long-term rather than a short-term phenomenon. The growth in numbers, fall in employment and accumulation of cases pushed the budget for income related benefits for lone parents to £6.8 billion in 1994. The total cost of benefits for lone parents (means-tested and non-means-tested, and including Child Benefit) came to £8.5 billion, or approximately 9 per cent of the social security budget. This shadows American experience, where the 30 per cent of the recipients of Aid to Families with Dependent Children for more than eight years account for almost two-thirds of the money paid out. (Again, long-term dependency is particularly characteristic of single mothers.)

By the end of the 1980s only 39 per cent of lone parents had ever received official maintenance from former husbands or partners and only 29 per cent had received regular payments. In 80 per cent of arrears cases, which used to be dealt with by the Department of Social Security, nothing was recovered. In 1993 the Child Support Agency came into operation to pursue absent fathers to recoup some of the costs of state support.

Decreasing maintenance has accompanied the increasing casualisation of relationships. Divorced mothers were the most likely to receive maintenance (40 per cent in 1989), and never married mothers the least (14 per cent in 1989) and then at very low levels. Single mothers are less likely to know who or where the father is, and to want maintenance. This is not surprising as fathers whose children are born outside marriage are less likely to be involved in every way and, when relationships end, are less likely to pay support or maintain contact. The marriage bond facilitates involvement with children in all dimensions of parenting, both for the duration of a relationship and if the couple split up, compared to where there has only been cohabitation.[11]

If 60 per cent of lone parents had fallen to below half average income by the 1990s, compared with 19 per cent in 1979, this increase is entirely accounted for by more dependence on Income Support. (It has to be borne in mind that the percentage of couples with children below half average income also trebled from 8 per cent to 23 per cent over the same period, particularly as labour and housing markets turned against them.)

Maintenance has fallen, but as the growth in the numbers of pre-school children in lone-parent households has risen dramatically, from just over 2 in 10 to 4 in 10, and young mothers with small children are less likely to work, this was bound to have an important impact on employment. Moreover, a third or more of the decline in workforce participation can be accounted for in terms of the disincentives of the benefit system, particularly as this has protected recipients from the soaring cost of housing borne by the working population over the 1980s.[12]

Poor parent, lone parent?

Child poverty is often identified as not only intrinsic to, but exclusive to, lone parenthood. Lone parents are invariably described as running "a higher risk of poverty ... compared with many other family types", as Jo Roll puts it in the 1992 Report to the European Commission.[13] (One assumes that she means the two-parent or conjugal family—it is unclear who the "many other family types" are.) Lone parents always suffer "greater financial hardship", according to the National Children's Bureau.[14] This suggests that poverty and lone parenthood are synonymous, or that lone parents are by definition poor.

The notion of lone parent poverty usually leads to the claim that the social security system treats lone parents unfavourably compared with married parents. For example, Joan Brown speaks of "poverty among one-parent families which arises out of deficient social security provisions".[15] These provisions are indicted for their inadequacy in being built on a two-parent norm which makes lone parents an anomaly, so that little account is taken of them. But once we treat poverty and single parenthood as independent variables, what credence can we give to assumptions that lone parents are *the poor*, or the poorest of those with children? Moreover, is it true that the benefits system neglects lone parents, or is meaner towards them compared with two-parent families?

One benchmark for poverty is provided by comparing family incomes with minimum benefit levels for families of a similar size or composition.[16] Families with net resources below Supplementary Benefit/Income Support level are the poorest group. Here, married couples with children vastly outnumber lone parents with children at 190,000 compared with 90,000 in 1979, and 310,000 compared with 160,000 in 1989. When we consider the numbers of persons involved the difference increases (see Figure 2, p. 162).

The resources available to those who, for various reasons, are unwilling or unable to claim Income Support or Family Credit are only 64 per cent of those available to Income Support claimants, having fallen from over 70 per cent in 1981. Families may be below public assistance level because they do not claim Income Support or are ineligible because of employment which—in being casual or irregular—also disqualifies them from receiving Family Credit (the means-tested benefit for families with low net wages). Housing costs are another reason, since housing benefit is only available to those in rented accommodation and, if owner-occupiers are not on Income Support, they get no help with interest charges.

It is very misleading to identify the poor simply with those on Income Support where, indeed, the prevalence of lone parents is higher and increasing (although the proportion of couples tends to increase in years of high unemployment).

If we look at statistics showing the number of individuals whose household income lies below various proportions of the national average, then again, while a large proportion of lone parents may have low incomes, this does not mean that they constitute *the majority of the population with low incomes*. (An analogy helps: while all oaks are trees, most trees are not oaks.) Thus 42 per cent in the population with incomes in the bottom half of the income distribution in 1989 were in households comprising married couples and children, while only 10 per cent were in lone-parent households. The rest is made up of a miscellany of single people, childless couples and retired people.[17]

One new finding for 1990/1 was the over-representation of couples with children in the bottom 10 per cent of the income distribution, where they made up almost half of the total group, or 49 per cent, while lone parents made up only 11 per cent (see Figure 3, p. 163). (A family type is over-represented or under-represented if the income group contains a higher or lower percentage of the particular family type than is found in the population as a whole.) In 1979 couples with children had accounted for 41 per cent of this group—a remarkable rise in a short period (see Table 1.5, p. 159).

Benefits Out Of Work

Despite protestations of the neglect and marginalisation of lone parents by the benefits system, Income Support and, even more,

Family Credit (aimed at the working poor) are now largely understood, and developed as services for a lone-parent clientele. The unemployed or low-paid two-parent family has become almost irrelevant.

As lone parents are exempt from the requirement to seek work, the extent to which benefit levels might erode work incentives did not arise when their public assistance entitlements were drawn up. They did relatively well out of the changes of 1980 (following the 1978 Social Assistance Review) compared with unemployed families. The higher rate for adults (previously restricted to the old and disabled and about 27 per cent higher than the ordinary rate) was extended to all not required to register for employment. This was precisely to provide an *alternative* to employment for lone mothers of dependent children.

Since the Fowler reforms, under 18s have not been entitled to claim Income Support and a reduced rate of £34.80 in 1993-4 applies to those aged 18-24. For a lone parent, however, the full adult rate of £44.00 applies. Two single, unemployed people had £88.00 between them, compared with £69.00 for a married or cohabiting heterosexual couple. All families had a *family premium* of £9.65, with *an extra premium for single parents* of £4.90. Adding allowances for a child under 11 and another aged 11-15 gave a couple £115.85 per week and a single parent £95.75. If the lone parent had an unemployed boyfriend, they drew a total of £139.75 (or £130.55 if he was under 25). Moreover, when they claim separately, the benefit of one cannot be reduced to pay the other's debts. Terry, who is paying off accumulated rent, electricity, gas and poll tax arrears from his Income Support, relies on his girlfriend, who gets Income Support as a lone parent:

> Whereas the income from his 'fiddle jobs' was variable, Claire's income was regular. Their entitlement to benefit was assessed separately as Claire was officially living on her own while on the council's waiting list ... In practice she spent most of the time at Terry's flat and shared her income with him.[18]

For a couple on Income Support the first £5.00 of earnings per person is ignored for benefit purposes, after which their allocation is reduced pound for pound. They must spend two years entirely out of work before this exemption is increased to £15.00 between them. For a single parent the first £15.00 of earnings is disregarded from the beginning of the benefit period, creating a disregard which is three times larger than that allowed to the father of a family. A woman operating as a child minder has two thirds of her gross income counted as expenses and ignored completely. Those on Income Support are normally entitled to housing benefit to cover rent, or mortgage interest is paid. Moreover, they were exempt from 80 per cent of the community charge (or poll tax) and claimants are now completely exempt from the new council tax. Among the 'passport benefits' available are free school meals, milk and vitamins for pregnant women and for each child under five. For mothers on Income Support or Family Credit, a maternity payment of up to £100 is available to help pay for things for the new baby. Families getting Income Support or Family Credit are also entitled to free prescriptions, free dental treatment, free sight tests, and vouchers for glasses and refunds of travel costs to and from hospital for NHS treatment. There are also School Clothing Grants, School Uniform Grants, Maintenance Grants for the over 16s, and University/Polytechnic Interview Expenses available from local authorities for those on means-tested benefits. Contributions towards school trips, courses and lessons and other, often substantial, 'voluntary contributions' that parents now have to make for educational purposes are waived.

It is useful to compare living standards of lone parents and couples with children on basic benefit. Research by the Family Budget Unit puts a low-cost budget (excluding rent) for two adults and two children under 11 at £141.40 compared to £110.41 for a lone parent in January 1993, while their benefit entitlements were respectively £105.00 and £85.60—a greater shortfall in the case of the couple, even allowing for the Unit's comparatively mean allocation for two adults. Work on childrearing costs shows how lone parents can afford somewhat more than couples with children.[19] Analysis of the impact of the 1980 Social Security Act showed how this left unemployed families worse off than lone parents, and more likely to report financial hardship, debts and difficulties in making ends meet. In the wake of the 1986 legislation, researcher and lone-parent advocate Jane Millar conceded that analysis continued to show lone mothers to be better off than families with unemployed fathers.[20]

While legal obligations on local authorities under Part III of the 1985 Housing Act to arrange permanent accommodation for the intentionally homeless who fall into a priority need category did not distinguish between one- or two-parent households, lone parents have been able to qualify for help in being both pregnant women (or people with dependent children), and *"people who are vulnerable* owing to old age, physical or mental ill-health *or some other special reason"* (emphasis added). This is probably the reason for the doubling, between 1974 and 1989, of the proportion of single mothers living alone to 73 per cent.

Depending somewhat on the interpretation of the local authority, a couple on a long waiting list for local authority housing might improve their (otherwise almost non-existent) chances if the woman became pregnant and the man deserted. Some authorities have turned their responsibilities into a housing policy that essentially provides only for lone parents. A sample of 40 representative authorities in 1993 showed that lone parents made up 41 per cent of acceptances under homelessness legislation. However, there are complaints from lone-parent representatives that, as suggested by the Housing Allocation Survey, there is still a tendency in some areas for lone parents to be offered slightly smaller properties than families. Because couples with one child are more likely to be allocated three-bedroomed properties, the accusation is that the expansion of this family type is more readily accepted compared to the lone parent's.[21]

Benefits On Low Pay

Social security benefits are also an important source of income for lone parents in work: more than a half of those in employment supplement part-time earnings in this way.

Family Credit as a supplement to wages had its origin in the 1970s (as Family Income Supplement) when the tax burden began to shift at the expense of families and downwards onto the lower paid, thus leading to family poverty and growing disincentives to work. Assistance for the out of work has to include subsistence allowances for any dependent children. This creates an incentives problem if no similar allowances, or far smaller ones, are made for the waged, whether by child tax allowances, family allowances, or goods and services in kind. This unemployment trap effect increases with the size of the family, and the 'ceiling of relief' is more likely to rise through the 'floor of wages' for the lower paid. The effect is enhanced if, as people lose their entitlements and incur work-related expenses, taxes and National Insurance contributions are imposed as well. The trap deepens as the benefit rate rises in relation to the net wage rate. It must be borne in mind that the overlap can occur, and leave people worse off employed than unemployed, even where benefit levels may be more or less inadequate to cover basic living costs.

In the 1940s and 1950s the income which a family was allowed to keep (given personal tax allowances, plus tax relief for children as well as family allowances) was a lot higher than out of work benefits. An aspect of the traditional principle of ability to pay was that the income necessary for the subsistence of the earner, and any dependants, should not be taxed away, nor taxes imposed on those without a surplus to meet these. Otherwise taxation becomes an instrument of poverty.

As it began to be just this by the 1970s the problem was tackled with means-tested relief to top-up the earnings of poorer working families. Other income-related benefits, like rate rebates, community charge benefit or council tax benefit and housing benefit, have been added for those on low incomes to meet the cost of local taxes and decontrolled rents. Since these reliefs are withdrawn as earnings rise, the effect is to undercut the rewards of effort.

It is when we consider the overall effect of all taxation, rents and means-tested benefits on final income that the magnitude of the disincentive effect becomes apparent. A couple with two young children with gross earnings of £55 per week saw £121.50 per week. If they grossed £100 per week, they had £124.76, or £3.26 more for a rise of nearly 100 per cent in initial earnings. If they grossed £150, they had £126.77. About 97p in the pound is taken away as they extend their working hours, and at some points on the income scale it is over 100p. Only when earnings reached £195 in 1993/94 was this loss 34p in the pound. However, at the exit point from the means-tested system, people become ineligible for everything from the maternity grant to free prescriptions and dental treatment. Families are likely to suffer a considerable overall loss unless there is a sharp rise in earnings to compensate for the withdrawal of 'passport benefits'.

While Family Credit is related to the number and age of children in the family, it is not related to the number of adults. This combines the 'poverty trap' with a pronounced 'marriage trap'. Lone parents get as much Family Credit as a two-parent family and, with a universal One-Parent Benefit (£6.05 in 1993/94) on top of the ordinary child benefit, this means more net income to support fewer people. With one child under 11 and one over 11, this gave one parent with a net wage of £70 a total of £164.55 in 1993/94, with £70.40 Family Credit, plus £24.15 child and one-parent benefit. A two-parent family had £158.50. With a net wage of £100, a lone parent got £173.55 and two parents £167.50. On £150 it was £188.55 to £182.50.

Taking other benefit adjustments and outgoings into account (e.g. local taxes and their rebates, rent, housing benefit, etc) the lone parent with two small children, on a gross wage of £150, ended up with £135.31 compared to the family's £126.77.

If a man lives with his family, all his income counts against its Family Credit. If he leaves, part of his contribution is 'extra' to the mother's entitlement. Where relationships are kept 'off the books', all contributions from men will be in addition to the mother's earnings and her Family Credit. The highest estimates for numbers of lone parents come from benefit claim statistics, around 1.4 million for 1991, and the lowest, of 1.16 million, from the Family Expenditure Survey, which interviews a cross-section of the public at home, and is therefore more likely to be accurate.[22] Of course, this applies to mothers on Income Support as well. In *Hard Times?*, Elaine Kempson and colleagues[23] describe the familiar arrangement where a separated mother or one in a 'loose long-term arrangement' agrees to forgo regular 'official' maintenance in exchange for undeclared financial provision on top of her Income Support. Both parties gain. The man does not have to pay so much and has direct control of his payments, while the mother gets more, since none of it counts against her means-tested entitlements.

There is a lenient, and largely unenforceable, cohabitation rule. To be treated as husband and wife for benefit purposes, both partners must not have any other home where they normally live. A sexual relationship is not sufficient to disqualify a mother from receiving full benefits and neither is a steady boyfriend who 'stays over' or a 'visiting' man. All payment or contributions in kind, whether food, meals, clothes, tobacco, etc, are ignored for benefit calculations.

Similarly, if the claimant sub-lets her home to a 'tenant', part of the income is ignored (the first £20 a week plus 50 per cent of the balance, or higher if heating is provided). If a woman is part of a *bona fide* couple, all this would come from income that is set against benefit. There may be no allowance made in the Family Credit system for mortgage costs but, by the same token, nothing is subtracted if someone outside the family pays. Thus, if an ex-husband pays the mortgage (a common form of divorce settlement), the money is not counted as family income as it would be if the couple live together. Hazel is a divorcee:

> She was a nursery nurse ... and earned about £11,000 a year. She also received Child and One-Parent Benefit totalling £124 a month as well as Family Credit of £133 a month. Hazel's husband paid the mortgage (£340 a month). ... She saved between £150 and £200 a month.[24]

Who's Caught in the Unemployment and Poverty Traps?

Incentives problems are intrinsic to means testing and no system has ever been devised which avoids them. People are continually led on by the mirage of 'targeting'—the idea that you can restrict benefits to the 'needy', or 'truly needy'—some class of victims of disadvantage immune to disincentives. But as soon as you subject benefits to income tests certain constraints take over. Either the amount must be very low, or that withdrawn from each £ must be very high as earnings rise, or so many people are eligible that the programme becomes less selective.

Claims that the unemployment trap uniquely, or especially, affects lone parents have eclipsed previous concerns with the way that fathers, particularly if they had two or more children, are more likely to be long-term unemployed than men with smaller families, as well as the fact that women whose husbands are unemployed are twice as likely to be unemployed themselves, since their earnings wipe out the couple's benefit.

The last time the incentives question in two-parent families received serious attention was in 1986, when a Green Paper on the *Reform of Personal Taxation*[25] criticised the system then in force where a man with a family got 1½ tax allowances (one personal allowance plus the married couple's allowance), compared to a two-earner couple's 2½ tax allowances, and argued for an enlarged personal allowance, whereby spouses who did not have enough income to set against their own allowance might transfer the balance to their partner. Since a rise in tax allowances raises the net income of married men in employment, it would increase work incentives. This was headed off amidst protests that easing economic pressures on two-parent families might be a disincentive for mothers to work.

Non-means tested allowances for dependants, which are not lost as earnings rise, mitigate the poverty trap. However, the only such allowance for two-parent families on Family Credit is Child Benefit, while lone parents also have One-parent benefit and a right to keep £15 maintenance (and all maintenance if they earn enough to exit from Family Credit). While lone-parents with mortgages may find it hard to achieve an income in work that matches their Income Support entitlements, this is within the reach of those on Family Credit who are receiving mainten-ance, but impossible for two-parent families. Couples' incomes actually fall if those with mortgages move off Income Support. Not surprisingly, even lone parents without qualifications were twice as likely to work, and three times as likely to work full-time, if they received regular maintenance payments, according to the 1991 Department of Social Security/Policy Studies Institute Survey. This has given a fillip to plans to increase the volume and regularity of maintenance payments, and the disregard of maintenance for benefit purposes. No comparative disregard has been suggested for men with families to increase their work incentives and the provision they might make for their families, and no question of the flagrant unfairness towards low-income, working couples has been raised.

In practice, one way that couples might override the traps has been through Invalidity Benefit claims, if there is some disability that can be used to qualify. As Invalidity Benefit is not means tested, a wife or husband can work without affecting their spouse's claim to this additional income. (The rapidly increasing numbers claiming Invalidity Benefit has led to a recent tighten-ing of criteria.) Another ploy is to qualify for maximum Family Credit when earnings are at their lowest and then to increase them rapidly, with overtime or a second job, before the six monthly reassessment is up, when earnings can be dropped again to re-qualify for another six months.

As Alan Marsh and Stephen McKay report in *Families, Work and Benefits*, Family Credit is a comparatively successful benefit for lone parents. The take-up rates are 70 per cent of those eligible and they typically gain £30 a week over Income Support.

In contrast, take-up rates are low for couples, and stand at less than half of those entitled. Given that the amount which couples get is smaller considered in relation to the number of adults, the work incentive effects of Family Credit are very limited. Families who try it are likely to fall back on Income Support.[26] Many lone parents have council accommodation, so that housing benefit continues to pay rent as they go to work. In contrast, more unemployed families have mortgage arrears and other debts which they carry with them into low-paid work, where they will increase since only Income Support pays for mortgage interest.

To give more encouragement to lone parents to earn, and switch from Income Support to Family Credit, the number of hours needed to qualify for Family Credit was reduced to 16 hours a week in 1992-93. The promise of the equality lobby was that the policy of 'giving more benefit to get off benefit', or full Family Credit for part-time work, would ease lone parents into the labour market, where they would graduate to remunerative full-time work, leaving means-tested assistance behind them and saving the government money.

This move to ease the unemployment trap is one of two recent and major enhancements of the marriage trap. If, for example; a lone parent worked part-time for a net wage of £80 for 20 hours in 1993-94, her Family Credit for two children, one under and one over 11, plus her child and one-parent benefits, brought this to £167.55. With £15 of maintenance from the father, the total was £182.55. A man supporting a family, or a couple who are both working, might put in 40 hours for £160 per week to end up with £185.50. Two lone parents living together, whether as friends, lesbians or mother and daughter, and both working part-time, would end up with £335.10 per week.

After the problems of unemployed couples with children had been supplanted by the difficulties of the lone mother, held back by benefits from getting into the labour market, the poverty trap then became a dilemma facing the lone parent trying to *increase her earnings*. Thus, while it has become admittedly more lucrative to work 16 hours rather than none or 10 since 1992-3, the complaint remained that—considering the loss of benefits and time, plus the extra costs involved in working 32 or 40 hours —this was not likely to be attractive unless well paid, resulting in claimants 'sticking' at the high rate of Family Credit instead of on Income Support.

It is tempting to suggest that the "poverty trap could be addressed by allowing benefit recipients to earn a little on the side before their benefits are reduced" or even increase their income "to a decent—and predictable—level before pulling the welfare rug from under them".[27] This, of course, defeats the point of means-tested benefits as assistance for the needy. However, the Budget of November 1993 allowed up to £40 to be deducted from the earnings figure used to calculate the Family Credit payable from Autumn 1994, ostensibly for childcare costs, so that there will be a gain of up to £28 per week. Being exactly the sum which the National Council for One Parent Families asked for, then clearly, what the NCOPF asks for from the government is what it gets. As lone parents already received as much Family Credit as a couple plus one-parent benefit, this could be read as a way in which these costs were already recognised, as much as that no allowance was made for the second parent who provides childcare in the two-parent family. However the effect of this measure will be that the lone parent working part-time for £100 net with one child under and one over 11 will get approximately £198.65 compared to £172.69 for the couple on the same net wage in 1994-95. At a full-time wage of, for example, £150, the couple will still only get £187.69, while a lone parent at this net wage will receive £221.84. The disregard also applies to housing and council tax benefit. Taking all benefits, taxes and rents into account, a married couple with two small children earning £150.00 gross will end up with £130.66. On £200.00 gross it is still only £136.11. A single parent with two small children claiming her £40.00 disregards, with a gross wage of £150.00, ends up with £170.62. On £200.00 gross she will get £174.03. Even on a part time gross wage of £75.00 per week she will get £163.31.

Supposedly two parents can qualify for the childcare allowance, but they would need to have unusual patterns of earning. It is not designed with them in mind. It does not apply to any domestic division of labour where one parent cares for the children while the other earns, or they operate some kind of alternate shift arrangement. Significantly, the government's own tax/benefit tables do not consider it worthwhile to refer to them. If both parties had full-time jobs, their combined earnings might take them beyond Family Credit limits and thus the childcare allowance, no matter what their substitute care costs might be.

They would have to both work in very low-paid jobs, at the same time, with the child in third-party care. But while they are doubling up like this, the lone mother would get as much or more money as the couple with half their combined effort.

Off Means-Tested Benefits

All single parents are not on means-tested benefits because they are unoccupied or have low earnings. Those in more remunerative work are entitled to all the provisions available for two parents, which has included the married couple's allowance (renamed the special personal allowance for lone parents), plus one-parent benefit. Wage for wage, this has meant a higher net income than that of a one-earner two-parent family, and a higher standard of living once this income is related to the number dependent upon it. The discrepancy becomes that much greater given that, in local taxation, the trend has been to charge extra where the housing unit has more than one adult. The main earner for a two-parent family paid double the community charge (or poll tax) by the late 1980s and now, with the Council Tax, pays 25 per cent more as part of a couple.

Just counting income tax and national insurance (without mortgage or other non-standard tax reliefs), most groups saw a reduction in their direct tax burden between 1979 and 1993, with the exception of couples with children around average earnings or less. When we add in indirect taxes and local charges, families' tax burdens have generally increased at all levels, as those of singles have fallen significantly.[28] (See Appendix, p. 164). The situation has been brought about through rising national insurance contributions, which are offset by no allowance for dependants, and the way that local authority rates rose rapidly from the 1970s and then, with the poll tax, and now the council tax, couples have had to pay more than lone adults. By 1992/3 the married couple with two children on one main income paid 36.2 per cent of income in all taxes at average earnings, compared with 42.0 per cent for a single childless person.

Most important, since child tax allowances and family allowances were replaced by child benefit, as the only way of equalising tax liabilities specifically between those with and without the charge of children, this has been under continued threat, and frozen in value from 1987 to 1990. Then it became the turn of the Married Couple's Allowance. Originally worth half of the basic single personal allowance until frozen in 1990-91, the value would have been £2,400 in 1993-94, if it had been regularly uprated, instead of remaining at £1,720. The Married Couples Allowance may go to childless couples, but it also goes to every working family. Lone parents have experienced the same decline in the value of child benefit and the married couple's allowance as two-parent families, but they have received some protection from the transfer of the tax burden onto families in being both single adults and single parents (one-parent benefit was uprated faster than inflation in the 1980s).

However, taxation of families is accelerating sharply upwards in the mid-1990s. From all the tax changes (covering income tax, national insurance and VAT) set in motion by the budgets of 1993, one-wage couples at average earnings with two children lose 4.57 per cent of their income. A two-wage couple with children lose 4.26 per cent; a two-wage couple with no children lose 4.04 per cent; a single person loses 3.54 per cent and a single parent loses 2.51 per cent. Having been frozen for several years, the cash value of the marriage allowance declined even further as a result of the reduction in relief to the 20 per cent rate of tax, instead of the main 25 and 40 per cent rates. It is now worth £344 instead of £430 or £688 at the higher rates. The situation will deteriorate even further when the value of the marriage allowance is reduced to £5 a week in 1995-96 as a result of a further cut in the relief to a 15 per cent rate of tax. Then, without the marriage allowance, a family provider will pay tax at the single rate on all income over £66, plus extra local tax.

Family benefits, services and exemptions have been remorse-lessly removed or reduced year by year since the 1970s, and the money saved from the reduction in the Married Couples Allowance will now pay off budget deficits swollen by both unemployment and the long-term rise in pension and one-parent benefit costs, while funding the increased payments made in the same 1993 budgets to the retired and lone parents.

The entry of feminist advisors into government with the Major administration removed all impediments to the Treasury's spiteful tradition of automatic opposition to any family benefiting measure at a time when government was looking for revenue from an uncomplaining source. The budgets of the 1990s represent the achievement of a persistent campaign to raise the taxation of fathers by removing all fiscal recognition of the responsibilities of marriage. Moves to ease the taxation of married couples with one principal earner have not only been staunchly opposed, but pressure for abolition of what had been labelled an 'unjustifiable' subsidy which might be put to better use, has come from officially sponsored and financed equal rights organisations and bodies dealing with family matters, as well as pressure groups sharing the feminist perspective. A common accompaniment of these demands has been calls for higher one-parent benefit and there has been some concern that working lone parents might lose the marriage allowance (in the form of the additional personal allowance) along with fathers, without general compensation. Indeed, while the National Council for One Parent Families supports the move to get rid of the tax allowance for the married, it sees "no justification" for also removing it from lone parents, and wants them to have both one-parent benefit and a lone-parent tax allowance on top of ordinary child benefit, while two parents only have the child benefit.[29]

But the concerted move to demolish the remaining fiscal support for men's contribution to families in the Chancellor's outright attack on this as an 'anomaly' in the November Budget of 1993 was accompanied by the emphatic development of means-tested benefits as an important aspect of a rapidly consolidating package for lone parents. Payments for out of home childcare for mothers on Family Credit were heralded as the beginning of a rapid expansion of government backed day care.

The Special Position

Lone parents end up with higher final incomes from any given wage than two-parent families, while those on Income Support get special premiums, and are the only category entitled to income security free of a work test. A neutral policy would be one which gave two-parent families similar support to lone parents, whereas the present system penalises the former.

Whilst it is true that some lone parents may have suffered violence or maltreatment, we have to remember that many lone mothers have also been responsible for initiating unilateral divorce proceedings and have been successful in claiming custody of their children. Alan Tapper complains about the obvious injustice of requiring couples who stay together to pay for the actions of those who:

> ... in the same circumstances, choose to separate. We can reasonably presume that all marriages are, at one time or another, subject to the sort of pressures which presently cause breakups ... It follows that the only fair form of family assistance is one which assists all families, those which separate and those which do not.

Divorce may be widespread and unpredictable, but it is not a reason to support only those who resort to it. After all:

> All parenting can be stressful and difficult—and those who manage to keep their families together may do so only by means of much effort and self sacrifice. To say this is not to say that those who succeed ... are better people ... only that what they have succeeded in doing is important and valuable, and that fairness or 'neutrality' requires some recognition of this. Society, though it does have a role in supporting all families, has no obligation to subsidise family breakdown.[30]

However, it has become an article of faith that lone parents are a particularly disadvantaged group. The Finer Report spoke of their occupying a 'special position' so that they required not just *as much* money as two-parent families but *more*, both in that one person must cover two people's functions and because of the existence of 'extra needs'.[31] Yet while this has become "part of the political language about one-parent families", the extra needs have been poorly identified.[32] The evidence suggests that, far from facing extra costs, lone parents, at any given level of income, enjoy a somewhat higher standard of living than two-parent families (see Appendix, p. 164). Specialists on the subject of women and benefits like to illustrate the way in which men are burdensome to the household by making much of the finding that lone mothers feel economically better off and more 'in control' than married women, not just because only they are spending the money but because they are the only adult using facilities. They can 'individualise collective expenditure' as the only consumer of what they pay for. With no one else turning on the light or drawing water, "savings made in this way were not absorbed by the expenses incurred by their partner."[33]

The justification for needing *as much* as two-parent families rests on the argument that the expenses of running a home do not change when there is one adult less: meals still have to be prepared, the home lighted, heated and cleaned, etc. Thus the same Family Credit as a couple, the same help for housing costs, whether as mortgage interest relief, or housing benefit, and the same amount of money exempt from tax is needed.

The view that lone parents need *more* than two-parent families stems from claims that a mother must, for example, pay workmen to do window cleaning, decorating, maintenance, gardening and so forth, which would otherwise be done by a husband. Moreover, they cannot shop around or exploit the economies of scale open to two parents and have to buy more expensive food. In turn, they have child care costs, not only when working, but going out socially (assuming that married parents do not go out together). Thus, the replacement costs of the second parent's labour tends to be counted while that of their keep is excluded. In practice the child's age, as well as the hours and type of parental work and the type of facility used, mean that costs will vary enormously (and may not exist), while the half of the couple providing care in a family always has to be fed, clothed, housed, entertained and generally provisioned.

Nevertheless the conclusion that the 'extra' expenditure of lone parents is "equal to or even exceeds the saving of not maintaining the other parent",[34] resulted in One-Parent Benefit—justified in the Fowler review of benefits in 1985 as a contribution towards the "additional costs faced by lone parents in bringing up children alone."[35] Since, where two parents provide services and support through the sharing of household labour, this now incurs extra local tax, suggestions are that they both have some kind of taxable advantage or more capacity to pay than do single people, as well as being more costly to the community.

All of these reasons for the preferential treatment of lone parents have been increasingly subsumed to a drive to create greater equality of income between one- and two-parent families.[36] This is not to be understood in the way that horizontal equity was once understood, as parity in living standards between those with and without the charge of children and other dependants, at any particular level of original income. If it was, then it would be an argument for a more equitable treatment of two-parent families *vis-à-vis* the lone parent and against, for example, extra one-parent benefit or the higher rates of Family Credit in relation to numbers. Instead, this is understood in

terms of group outcome, or moving the lone parent into parity
with the *average* income for two-parent families. Moreover, the
suggestion is that this now means parity with the *two-earner*
family.

It is significant that the lone parent trying to improve her
earnings in the face of the high benefit withdrawal rates of the
Family Credit system is now compared, not to the low-paid
family man who faces an even steeper poverty trap, but to the
double earner couple or second earner in a family whose
combined income carries them well beyond means-tested assistance.[37] (Here, of course, with no subsidy to withdraw, people
have more of each pound earned.)

The Political Process

What is being created is the new 'family wage', tailored for lone
parents, in place of the old system of tax exemptions and
allowances which helped to maintain and rear children in the
two-parent family. It testifies to the way in which the various
functions of childrearing have lost recognition when performed in
the context of the conjugal family. Indeed, they have come under
concerted attack. For a man, the provider role has been persistently dismissed and derogated as outworn and unworthy in
being a drag anchor keeping women out of employment. By the
same token, no allowance is justified for the mother to care for
children at home, at least when she is part of a couple. In
contrast, no such odium attaches to the providing mother
striking out independently, so that a lone parent must be helped
in *Becoming a Breadwinner*,[38] as a noble endeavour of which she
can be justly proud, with wage supplements, job opportunities,
training and childcare assistance.

The trend away from universal recognition for dependants in
the tax and benefit system and the growth of means testing, and
the abandonment of family policy, in favour of the development
of relief for the needy and the 'casualties', has been facilitated
by this withdrawal of normative affirmation from the conjugal
family. The rearing of children has been reduced to the status
of just another individual expenditure choice made by consumers
in the marketplace, somewhat equivalent to the upkeep of a car.
And if, in supporting a wife bringing up children, the husband
is simply providing himself with personal services, then it is
possible not only to withdraw all allowances for marital responsi-

bilities, but actually to tax these on the basis that they are a benefit for the earning partner.

As with the sharp rise in the number of elderly people in relation to the declining numbers of the young, the increase in lone parents might suggest that the pressure on resources involved would make their situation unfavourable compared to the intact family, since the cost of their support to the state is so much greater. Exactly the opposite has occurred and demographic developments have not only failed to prevent this trend, but facilitated it, since public decisions are influenced by the power of interest groups, and power is partly a function of size. Moreover, the larger the role of transfers going to growing groups and the bigger the role of government in guaranteeing these, so, paradoxically, the more advantageous it is to be in an expanding dependency group. We can see a multiplier effect: support for lone parents increases their numbers, while the supply of intact families falls as resources are transferred away from them.

The loss of basic, guiding convictions about the value of family life at policy making level has encouraged the occupation of this field by sectional interests, and the increasing tendency of the political process to give special treatment to those who are well organised, active, and sophisticated in pursuing a narrow set of interests.[39] The rise of lone parents generally, and their disproportionate reliance on an expanding means-tested and selective benefits system, has meant that what would be, anyway, an active pressure group, has been mobilised by women's rights and feminist interests. While leaders of lone- parent organisations have been recruited to the kitchen cabinets of Ministers with responsibility for 'women's issues', these have contained nobody with a brief for the conventional family. Instead, Chancellors have acquired advisors who urge them to its more speedy and complete plunder.

The more the state accommodates a client group, the less that government feels able to refuse and the more fearful it is of creating offence. No such group ever represents itself as anything but poverty-stricken, maligned, discriminated against, and generally put upon. It also pays to be exquisitely sensitive to anything that can be construed as insulting, critical or uncaring, and to put on the most extravagant display of outrage, as this leads to compensatory or propitiatory awards.

The point has not been lost on some feminist ideologues that the consequences of greater public economic provision for lone mothers is that dependency shifts from men to the state, creating what they have called a 'state patriarchy'. This makes use of the old Marxist critique of provision for the poor under capitalism as just another means of social control; enforcing the work ethic and damping down revolutionary ardour. But more perceptive, given the present hold of interest groups over political decision making, are those who see the state as a resource to exploit, rather than a mechanism of control, and realise that the "main opportunities for women to exercise power today inhere precisely in their 'dependent' relationships with the state".[40]

It has been remarked that the "feminisation of the state launches a new offensive in the gender war. It is now an orthodoxy that one of the primary duties of the state is to protect women's interests against men's."[41] As typically phrased by Polly Toynbee, what the state "can do is shape a society that makes a place for women and children as family units, self-sufficient and independent" if they are not to "suffer needlessly".[42] Here, it is the attempt by men to provide for families which is not only made to account for lone-parent poverty but also for family poverty generally, which is construed as women's poverty. This claim is prominent among the many arguments surrounding the role or relation of lone parenthood to poverty, and they deserve examination more than rhetoric.

Perpetuating Poverty

Summary: *Family poverty was falling and child welfare was rising until the early 1970s. Since then these trends have gone into reverse. This has accompanied the growth in numbers of lone-parent families and the 'flight from marriage'. Much of the growth in poverty affects two-parent families, and there are increasing numbers of working poor as well as unemployed. Poverty may be the cause of family breakdown as well as its consequence: the shift of the burden of taxation onto married couples with children makes it more difficult to form and maintain families. However, children brought up in households where no one is employed (either in one- or two-parent families) are more likely to be unemployed themselves, having never acquired 'right' attitudes towards work. The children of lone parents are further disadvantaged by the lower educational attainment associated with fatherless families, which will in turn affect their earning potential. The 'children of divorce' are down wardly mobile. They are less likely to marry, more likely to divorce if they do marry and, in the case of females, more likely to become lone parents in their turn.*

Lone Parent, Poor Parent?

IT HAS BECOME almost axiomatic that lone parents are, by definition, poor, and that poverty in the working age population is predominantly a lone-parent problem. It is a short step to the next assumption, which is that rising poverty must be somehow tied to, if not directly attributable to, increasing lone parenthood. It is the task of this section to look a little more closely at whether lone parenthood can account for poverty in society and, particularly, what credence can be given to influential versions of a 'feminisation of poverty' thesis, associated with both establishment feminists and writers of the 'new right'.

Because of the nature of childrearing, a connection may seem obvious. Lone parents have dual responsibilities. They lack the support of another parent, where the family functions as an economic unit in which earnings can be distributed to those who are caring for children. They then go on to perpetuate their poverty, because parenthood, particularly early in life, damages career growth and economic security. Moreover, a £ or $ of income-related benefit does not simply add a £ or $ to a needy person's income, but creates incentives for individuals to change their behaviour to continue qualifying, so that the size of the poverty population may be increased by welfare dependency. In cases of divorce, many men simply do not have the resources to support sets of children from serial marriages. Therefore we have to ask if what appears to be an economic problem might be rather the economic manifestation of a social phenomenon. Of course it might be argued that, if lone parenthood is a potent source of poverty, perhaps there should be less of it. This view tends to be marginalised as:

> ... a refusal to accept the realities of life. It is like having a weather policy which, instead of providing people with umbrellas, tries to stop the rain from falling.[1]

Growing Child Poverty

It is undeniably true that, in the same years that lone parenthood has ascended so steeply, all measures of child or family poverty have also been on the rise. This reverses a long-term historical trend, with family poverty consistently dropping, and child welfare increasing. By the 1950s sociologists in Britain reported that subsistence poverty among families had almost vanished and the same was true for America, as the 1940s figure was halved by the end of the 1950s and halved again by the 1970s.

By then, however, contrary currents were in evidence. The percentage of children at incomes below the contemporary average rose from 71 per cent to 75 per cent between 1979 and 1991—although the numbers fell because there were fewer children—and those below half the average rose from 10 per cent to 31 per cent.[2]

On a benefit measure nearly a third of all children, and 45 per cent in three-child families, were living in families that were below, on, or within 140 per cent of public assistance levels by the mid-1980s. Furthermore, while recession helped to bring millions below the thresholds, the boom of the late 1980s failed to take as many out. Welfare dependency has also seen a big growth, as a large-scale pauperization of procreation has occurred. The proportion of families with children (one- and two-parent) drawing one or more means-tested benefits grew from 8 per cent to 30 per cent between 1979 and 1992. Shockingly, 30.1 per cent of under fives were in families receiving Income Support in 1993 and 7.5 per cent were in families drawing Family Credit. For children aged 12 to 15 it was 20 per cent and 8.6 per cent.[3]

Feminisation of Poverty Mark 1: the Result of Family Breakdown

In his 1984 book *Losing Ground* Charles Murray first coupled the upsurge in youth unemployment, dropout from the labour force, welfare dependency, family dissolution and illegitimacy—that "demographic wonder, without precedent in the American experience"[4] and the way in which the numbers of the poor stopped shrinking in the early 1970s and began to grow. By the mid-1980s one in four children (one in two blacks) were living in poverty using the American definition. (This measures poverty independently of both the public assistance line, or average income, so that the line falls at three times the cost of a frugal diet). People in female headed families were a growing proportion of the non-aged poor, constituting over a third by 1980. They were also more likely to be persistently poor (61 per cent of those who had been under the poverty line for 10 years or more in the Michigan Panel Study of Income Dynamics were in female headed families by the mid-1980s). Moreover, on top of the fact that almost 40 per cent of never married mothers have been spending 10 or more years on public assistance, the children of welfare-dependent mothers are more likely to become welfare dependent themselves.[5]

Those like Charles Murray who place a particular responsibility for poverty on the retreat from marriage see this as precipitated and facilitated by the perverse incentives of welfare. This began in America when, with the declaration of the 'War on Poverty' in 1964, the following decade saw a growth in public assistance far exceeding the real increase in per household income. There were expanded rights and entitlements and more liberal interpretation of entitlements, together with reduced stigma attached to being on welfare. Originally Aid to Families with Dependent Children (AFDC) was designed for widows, but changes in the qualifying rules brought it within the range of more lone parents. All the mother had to do was not work and not marry an employed man. It converted the low-income working husband into a financial handicap, as a lone mother could receive more from the government than from the earnings of her potential husband. As the family was eligible for an expanded package of help as a result of the father's actual or staged desertion, this could mean an immediate increase in economic well-being. (This has been reined in somewhat since the 1970s and more states have given AFDC-UP, where the father can join the mother to receive public assistance, but only so long as he does not work.)

However, Murray sees short-term gain leading to long-term loss. What may have seemed a tempting option at the time precluded any advance, and "any teenager who has children and must rely on public assistance to support them has struck a Faustian bargain with the system that neatly ensures that she will live in poverty the rest of her days." His "set of modest requirements" for avoiding poverty urge people to get married and stay married, get a job—even if initially low paid—and stay in it and, "whatever else she does: a poor woman who wishes to get out of poverty ought not to have a baby out of wedlock."[6]

Feminisation of Poverty, Mark 2: The Patriarchal Plot

Where feminists are concerned, the lone parent is not at risk of poverty because one person has all the functions that would otherwise be distributed in a group. Instead, the family itself and its division of labour are "fundamentally the main cause of the high risk of poverty among lone mothers."[7] Their plight must be put in the context of women's overall power and economic position, where it "mirrors and then concentrates" their difficulties as "economically disadvantaged compared to husbands and fathers".[8]

It all sounds as if women have no choice as to whether to marry and have children: social conditioning, poverty and social pressure leave no option. This leads to the claim that "One of the many advantages of being male is that it is easier to opt out of the obligation to maintain than it is to opt out of the unwritten obligation to care".[9] However, childless married women who were full-time workers in the sample of 33-year-olds for the National Child Development Study[10] earned exactly the same—

£6.60—when measured on a gross median hourly basis, as single men. The overall statistical average for women's wages at around 79 per cent of men's is, of course, often used to demonstrate that women are still paid 'unequal wages'. These are, and have long been, illegal, and any woman doing the same or similar job to the man on the desk or bench next to her, or at the same grade, is paid exactly the same. The gap is explained by other factors. Prominent among them is married men's increased work effort. Another is the expansion in service sector jobs. These pay less than the manufacturing ones they are replacing and they disproportionately employ women, at a time when women are an expanding section of the labour force.

On the understanding that major wage inequalities and employment bars still exist, the "assumption that men are financially responsible for families" is seen to be at "the root of women's disadvantage in the labour market". This "makes it so hard for women alone to provide adequately for themselves and their children."[11] Society also assigns the care of children to their mothers when it could equally arrange for them to pass their babies to a child-rearing agency—so that its view of lone mothers as 'mothers' exposes them to the poverty "assigned by subsistence level benefits".[12] As Polly Toynbee complains, hundreds and thousands more women each year "lean on the state, in a life of poverty, despair and misery" because they were brought up "as relatively helpless dependent creatures, born to lean on others".[13]

This analysis, which is basically Marx's theory of class exploitation applied to the family, informs reports for the European Commission and those which flow from public or publicly funded bodies like the Equal Opportunities Commission and prominent research institutes, the literature of pressure groups and children's charities, and the 'independent' Commission of Social Justice, set up by the Labour Party. Claims are made that lone mothers only make manifest a general impoverishment of women that is concealed in families, or 'hidden in the household', where women are 'rendered invisible' in official and unofficial estimates of the incidence of poverty. Insofar as married women derive their livelihood from access to income received by men in the first instance, this economic dependence goes to maintain women's subordinate position in society.

Since income received as a result of a transfer brings dependency by definition, its receipt can leave women with a sense of obligation towards their partner. For example, income transfers between partners may be conditional, implicitly or explicitly, on marital fidelity or supplying 'unpaid' domestic labour and childcare.[14]

But, at the same time as women are said to be enslaved by dependence upon the male breadwinner, so his financial provision is described as a 'myth', as men spend all the money on themselves or use their oppressive provider role to *avoid* supporting others:

Part of this asymmetrical power arrangement is ... that, because of their 'breadwinner' status and generally high incomes, men are able to legitimate ... a claim to greater control over household resources and a right to appropriate or retain for their own personal use income which might otherwise be shared between all household members.[15]

As the only income available to many wives is said to be Child Benefit,[16] this suggests want on a massive scale (it being only £10 per week for the first child and £8.10 thereafter in 1993/94), particularly since it is implied that men only pay for housing, heating, water, etc., for themselves. Men are also blamed for handing over earnings because this leaves women to 'manage their poverty'. After all, in around half of households earnings are pooled and managed by the woman, who allocates the man his spending money. This, and the 'female whole wage system', in which all earnings are handed to the woman, are most common at low income levels. (Only about 20 per cent of households have a 'housekeeping allowance' with the man managing the balance and this is more usual at high-income levels.)[17] Elaine Kempson and colleagues found that low-income couples concentrated money-management in the hands of the party who was considered the more careful with money, which was generally the woman. Control of decision making over money matters was more divided although, again, women were in control when there was unemployment, even if the husband received the benefit.[18] Instances where a man used the control of finances to ensure that he had a significant share of the money for personal use were uncommon and linked with domestic violence. Here and elsewhere, it is more the refusal of men to accept a provider role that is related to patterns of domination, not the other way round.

Overall, and contrary to the interpretation now commonly given to it, this evidence suggests that there is little injustice in the income distribution in the family, and that what exists is insufficient to be the cause of the kind of privation, even virtual starvation, that is being alleged. Moreover, the issue is obfuscated by the way that women's poverty or deprivation often seems to amount to inadequate spending money or compensation for self-centred male consumption (on drinks or cars, for example), or a lack of resources for personal non-essentials.

But under every arrangement, women are seen to prevent or reduce the poverty, or add to the comparative comfort, of men and children, by budgeting scarce resources to their own cost. If we are accustomed to see much of what comprises an individual's standard of living as a matter of joint consumption, enjoyed by and contributing to the quality of life of all household members, this ignores the 'distribution of resources and needs'. Apparently, "nothing, whether it be work, money, help from relatives, food or time, is shared equally".[19] It is even alleged that women in families have unequal access to warmth, light and space at home.[20]

And even were there completely equal shares in anything from Grandma's time to room on the sofa, and the wattage from the light bulbs, this would not apparently reflect the way in which men and women derive unequal benefits from everything from food to consumer durables, with women always losing. Resources are also wasted by men on frivolous purposes, like using hot water or the bathroom for washing and shaving, in comparison with women responsible for childcare, washing clothes and cleaning the house. Anyway, joint consumption cannot serve the interests of all, since goods are 'gendered' and contribute to the living standards of men at the expense of women. However, if a more productive use of income gave women 'unlimited access to washing machines' or such like, this would rather facilitate servitude than increase consumption.[21]

As wage earners women "cushion their families from the impoverishing impact of male low pay",[22] and it is deplored how their wages "tend to be treated as household, rather than personal, income and ... simply reduce the calls on the man's income".[23] This implies that men are supposed to support the family alone, while still being regarded as oppressors because they are providers. In turn, women's unpaid and 'invisible labour' creates expectations that they "will do things for others, whether this involves caring for children, providing emotional support or washing socks".[24] Men advance through the ways that women are made to deprive themselves:

> ... women's unpaid labour ... helps to free their male partners ... from the time consuming constraints of domestic and caring activities, thereby enabling men to engage in paid employment and maintain or enhance their earning power relatively unfettered by home responsibilities.[25]

Evidence from the 1980s suggests that the consequent loss of earnings by wives in the childbearing years were still being offset to a not insignificant degree by the higher earnings of husbands (as these took on overtime, more responsibilities, second jobs, etc).[26] Of course, this only represents the average, and many men may not have been able to do this at all, or only to a minor extent. However, if women not engaged in child-rearing earn as much as men, and then the fall in their earnings as they bear children is, hopefully, accompanied by a rise in their husband's contribution, this would seem a remarkably co-operative arrangement—particularly considering how increasingly difficult this has become in an equal wage and opportunity labour market. Yet all is construed as an abuse, where men as breadwinners are "everywhere putting their interests before those of women"[27] and, providing themselves with services to exploit for their own advancement, they prevent women making their own money.

While it is claimed that time spent as a homemaker disadvantages women on their full return to the labour market, the effect on women's wage rates may be greatly exaggerated.[28] However, this is to be distinguished from calculations of the earnings loss of wives (or £224,000 as calculated by Heather Joshi in 1992) in the childrearing years. But here, as elsewhere, the concern is not with overall family resources, whoever provides them, but only those going direct to women from wages or the state as 'independent income'.[29] Otherwise, "Caring is what they do; poverty describes the economic circumstances in which they do it".[30] Some estimate that half of wives are in poverty because their own income is below public assistance level—irrespective of the family's economic status or their actual access to household resources.[31] Alternatively, they "could potentially have been in 'hidden poverty' if their husbands did not share their resources", where 'dependence' and 'hidden poverty'—if not synonymous—are different sides of the same corrupt coin:

> If resources are fully pooled 'hidden poverty' is averted but dependency is established. If the man's income is not shared, his partner may be in poverty, hidden by the unit aggregation, but will not be dependent upon him.[32]

Those working on the findings for 33-year-olds from the National Child Development Study characterise three-quarters of the young women as relying on transfers from their partners to maintain their living standards, by insisting that women must contribute at least 45 per cent of the household income, if they are not to be defined as dependent or in hidden poverty. But nearly a half are held to be below a 'self-sufficiency level' as well, in not having enough current income of their own to leave the relationship and support themselves, home and children, independently. Of course, many people would hardly be able to support themselves if they lost their jobs, or state pensions or benefits, or their investments failed. However, this raises the question of the usefulness of measurements of potential or hypothetical poverty. In many of these feminist analyses contradictions abound and no definition seems stable. The only consistency appears to be malice aforethought where, as Michelle Barrett and Mary McIntosh candidly admit, attacking men's provision for families "is a bit like an atheist attacking god the father: she wants to say it does not exist, that the false belief that it does has evil consequences and that even if it did exist it would not be a good thing".[33]

Where the Poor Come From

It happens to be far from the case that poverty largely manifests itself in the privations of lone parents. As we have seen in Chapter 1, poverty is increasingly *visible* in two-parent families. In the bottom 10 per cent of the British income distribution in 1991, 80 per cent of children had two parents, and 20 per cent were with lone parents. Indeed, 62 per cent of British children in the bottom half of the income distribution were in families headed by a full-time worker, while 35 per cent in the lowest 10 per cent income level had two parents and at least one full-time worker.

This picture is repeated in America where family poverty is often the poverty of the working poor, who made up 44 per cent of poor two-parent families in the mid-1980s. A majority, or 70 per cent, of American poor working household heads are married and white and, despite growing unemployment, the working poor became a fast-growing segment of America's poverty population, many of whom "could not keep a family out of poverty even if they worked 52 weeks at their current weekly earnings".[34] The earnings of a full-time, minimum wage worker fell 20 per cent short of the poverty line for a family of three, and 38 per cent for a family of four. In 1968 the same worker with a family of three would have been 20 per cent *above* the poverty line. The particular tragedy of the working poor is, as David T. Ellwood claims, that they ought to command our greatest sympathy and respect, yet we ignore their plight while we focus attention on single mothers who are on welfare.[35]

Child poverty used to be identified with big families, but in recent years it has grown while family size has fallen to the lowest ever recorded. If families become any smaller there will be no families left to talk about. Moreover, there have been more workers per family due to the increased labour force participation of married women. Measured by average, after tax, per capita income, families with children have become the lowest income group—below elderly households, single people and couples without children.

Those who have had a spectacular climb in wealth are without dependent children or requirement to work. British pensioners saw a rise for couples of 48 per cent in income between 1979 and 1991. Despite being a fast-growing dependent population, pensioners were no longer over-represented in the bottom income group in 1991 (constituting only 11 per cent, compared with 31 per cent in 1979 or, for pensioner couples only 6 per cent compared with 20 per cent). In contrast to those with children, pensioners' income growth is greatest at the lowest levels.[36] There were significant falls in the numbers having to supplement pensions with means-tested Income Support or living within 140 per cent of the public assistance line. The figures underestimate the drop, because of the considerable rise in pensioner numbers.

Similarly, the American elderly now have a higher living standard than working age people. One reason for the growing affluence is because entitlements have grown so much. The other is the considerable help in the child-rearing years which facilitated the accumulation of assets, not debts. In Britain, and much the same is true for America and Australia, there would have been everything from generous tax allowances for children and grants for higher education, school meal and travel subsidies, small mortgages or controlled rents, and much else besides that has since disappeared for younger generations.

It may reasonably be said that the poverty of children is a mirror image of that of the elderly where, since the 1960s, poverty has been transferred wholesale from the old to the young. Others who have participated disproportionately in British income growth are couples without children, who saw a rise of 42 per cent over the 1980s.[37]

Family Poverty and the Economy

Changes in living arrangements cause rises in poverty, but then so do other factors like the performance of economies and changes in taxation. Even without the upward pressure on poverty rates exerted by more lone parents, a significant rise in poverty would have occurred on both sides of the Atlantic.

The long-term data suggest that most poverty starts with income or job changes. One set of findings from a mass sample showed that family breakup accounted for 15 per cent of the total of poverty spells of five years or more that began for Americans in 1984. An equal amount was attributable to disablement and far more to declines in the labour force participation of the household head or other earners.[38] In turn, while welfare has had measurable effects on work effort, marriage and divorce (see Chapter 3), the changes in the labour supply and marriage rates that it induced were not enough to be the predominant cause of American poverty, compared to what it would have been without welfare.

Despite more dual earners, American family income was no higher, or even fell, in the 1980s compared to the late 1960s. The median income of couples under 30 with children fell 26 per cent between 1973 and 1986, or 6.2 per cent for those over 30 (couples without children saw rises of 2 per cent and 6.5 per cent respectively). Households with children—receiving little in the way of government transfers—are most affected by market conditions, while elderly households, receiving large transfers and insulated from market conditions, do well.[39]

In the past, stronger economies reduced poverty. At the same time, high levels of government support for families also had a big anti-poverty effect. However, from the 1970s, bouts of recession and industrial reorganisation, combined with the decline or elimination of tax-related and other measures of support, have eroded workers' ability to support their families on both sides of the Atlantic. (Nearly 75 per cent of the increased poverty of two-parent American families is accounted for by changes in market income and 25 per cent by increased taxes.)[40]

The Burden of Taxation

The birth of children always reduces earning potential while increasing expenditure. A family in Britain in 1993 with two young children needed 57 per cent more than a childless couple to maintain the same living standard.[41] Two adults and two small children needed a minimum of £337 a week to cover the basics of a modest living standard (as established owner-occupiers, outside London), compared to £240 for a bachelor with a new mortgage, or £151 if he was a tenant.

But as the tax burden has moved downwards, those with dependent children have been the hardest hit. The income tax threshold for a married man with two young children in Britain fell from 101.2 per cent of average male manual earnings to 34.9 per cent between 1950 and 1993-94. If we also take family allowances into account (setting them against tax), then the break-even point before which a married man with two small children paid no net tax was 124.5 per cent of average male manual earnings in 1950 (or 188.2 per cent for four children), but 63.7 per cent in 1993-94. For a single, childless person the tax threshold fell from 39.9 per cent to 23.3 per cent, or by 16.6 percentage points compared to the family's 66.3—a four-fold difference. Child Tax Allowance and the Family Allowance had been combined in Child Benefit by the 1980s, when they were both at their lowest points, and this was before the freezes of the 1980s further reduced the value of Child Benefit (by 23 per cent for second and subsequent children). This has been followed by the rapid reduction in value of the Married Couple's Allowance (see p. 20), and accompanied by the increases in other taxes, like national insurance contributions and local taxation, which impose a disproportionately heavy burden on family earners. Since the 1970s scarcely a year has gone by without a family exemption, benefit or service being removed or reduced.

Families have funded other people's benefits, as the continued expansion of the welfare state has been paid for by the primary welfare institution. As governments came to cut tax rates in the 1980s and 1990s, or create lower tax bands, while removing allowances (except those for seniority, which have been expanded), this has amounted to a redistribution of the tax burden onto those with family responsibilities and away from those without. Double income, childless couples and singles have been the main beneficiaries. This largely explains the paradox of increased taxation in a period of reduced tax rates. It is families who have had to pay for the extension of means-tested relief to bail out their own poor, when many families would not have fallen below the poverty line if their allowances had not been cut and extra charges imposed.

This all reflects the abandonment of the principle of ability to pay in taxation, which was traditionally related to both the level of income and the number of people dependent upon it. In its place is both a flattening of the national tax structure, regardless of the number of dependants, and the move towards charges, rather than exemptions, for dependants in the local tax system. Supposedly the system is neutral in paying no heed to people's differing family responsibilities, treating everyone as if they had none, but accompanying this is a complex means-tested system of relief for those whose income after taxes is insufficient to cover the subsistence costs of their families. General, or universal, recognition for the costs of dependants remove far more people from poverty than do means-tested transfers which, while purporting to aid those with low incomes, simply mean that the recipients lose less than they would otherwise have done after the depredations of taxation.

In Britain, particularly, mass welfare dependency, or a growing pauperization of procreation, is the expected outcome of a tax system ungoverned by the ability to pay and a benefits system based on 'need'. As government has concentrated on 'targeting the needy', so the iron law of welfare has been activated. This makes it difficult to reduce welfare dependency and child poverty at the same time. Means-tested and selective

benefits are administratively burdensome, initiative depressing
programmes designed to offset adverse economic outcomes, not to
enhance personal opportunities. The more adequate benefits are
to relieve poverty, the steeper they must decline in the face of
earnings, so the more they destroy the rationality of work—
unless they become far less selective. Then we get what Charles
Murray refers to as "broadening target populations", where
political expediency adds a new layer to the eligible population.[42]
Of course, benefits could be lowered to increase incentives, but
then they would be less adequate in reducing child poverty,
particularly if labour market conditions and taxation are
undermining family income at the same time.

America has seen a similar anti-family tax trend, with the
erosion of the value of exemptions for dependants, the zero
bracket amount and the earned income tax credit (for the
working poor). Rising payroll taxes, unadjusted for dependants,
rose automatically by 400 per cent between 1955 and 1985 to
pay for big pension increases. As these pushed young families
into poverty so, at the same time, the federal and payroll taxes
on a family of four at the poverty line rose from 1.3 per cent to
10.5 per cent between 1975 and 1985. In 1950 the average
family paid only 2 per cent of its income in federal taxes; by
1994 it was 24.5 per cent. When local and other taxes are
added, the figure rises to 37.6 per cent—remarkably similar to
the UK tax burden on the family. Singles, and couples with no
children, escaped most of this tax increase. As in Britain, cuts
in tax rates were largely irrelevant to families and the low paid.

The impact of tax and labour market trends on children were
greatly exacerbated by the way in which a declining proportion
of the federal budget was spent on the young. All spending on
children, from public assistance to education, to child and
maternal health care fell by 4 per cent over the 1980s as
spending on the elderly rose by 52 per cent. This prompted the
question of whether it was "fair to spend 22.9 per cent of the
federal budget on those over 65 (with a poverty rate of 4 per
cent to 12 per cent) but only 4.8 per cent on those under 18
(with a poverty rate of 17 per cent to 20 per cent)?[43]

There is some contrast with Britain in that the Tax Reform
Act of 1986 cut income tax on the low paid to its 1978 level by
expanding exemptions and the standard deduction, increasing the
Earned Income Tax Credit (to about 5 per cent of income for a

family of four at the poverty line) and abolishing some of the income tax privileges of the elderly. The Earned Income Tax Credit was further expanded in 1992, but taxes have continued to increase on middle incomes, and the changes do not affect the increasing burden of local and payroll taxes. Nor could they alleviate the effect of declining earnings, which have a bigger effect than in Britain.

One way that families try to meet rising costs is to push more labour onto the market, so that multiple earners have become important to transitions out of poverty. It is one reason why families have been more likely than lone parents to escape poverty, and underlines the increasing strain on couples as much as any numerical disadvantage of the lone parent. In a sample of 3,000 British families with net income below 140 per cent of the ordinary rate of public assistance, 35 per cent of two-parent families rose above this poverty line a year later, compared to 11 per cent of lone mothers. However, it was overwhelmingly those two-parent families with two earners who did so.[44]

Even more pointed is longitudinal American data showing how substantial changes in the household labour supply of other earners, apart from the head or wife, also have a strong relationship to transitions in and out of poverty for all families.[45] In America only about a fifth of the exits of lone mothers from public assistance are directly attributable to their own increased earnings.[46]

Welfare critics place great emphasis on the role of family breakdown in the rise of poverty, by giving prominence to the ability of two people to generate the income necessary to get over the poverty line, without querying why two earners are now needed. By 1981 it took about 1.3 earners to achieve the independent but lower level standard of living for four persons; 1.7 for a moderate level; and two full-time earners for the higher level.[47] In itself, this points to other developments besides family formation problems as causes of poverty.

It cannot be assumed that a mother and her children would not be poor had she not become a lone parent. Poverty may simply be reshuffled, as poor two-parent households break up and become poor lone-parent households. As family breakup coincided with only 22 per cent of the beginning of poverty spells for poor black American lone parents in the 1980s, and for 49 per cent of the white, clearly many of these women were coming from families or marriages where they were *already* poor or poorer.[48] Claims about how the majority of children being brought up in two-parent families escape poverty compared to a minority of those of lone parents, so often made in relation to the American statistics, are misleading. The situation may reflect the fact that family structure is as much a consequence as a cause of poverty. If poor lone parents had somehow been made to stay in or form two-parent families, this might simply raise the poverty rate for two-parent families instead.

But, for all that, if we just look at the beginning of poverty spells, this may lead us to underestimate the amount of poverty due to family change, however this is first brought about. We must also, as Robert I. Lerman explains, look ahead to the missing potential contribution of fathers. Thus:

> ... had the mother and father remained together, poverty begun before the household composition changed might not have continued, and poverty begun after the change might have been avoided.[49]

Low-income mothers who divorce are more likely to have stagnant incomes over the following years, compared to those who stayed married, and divorced, separated or never married fathers may be more likely to continue with low or no earnings compared to men living with a wife and children. In other words, there is more self-generating poverty.

The Cycle of Poverty

People do not just fall into poverty but also manage to climb out, even after a short period of time. However, lone parents may not be very successful in improving their circumstances whether their poverty is simply carried from a poor two-parent family into a poor one-parent family, or is the direct result of family breakup. (The most powerful predictor of time on American public assistance is marital status.) The sheer structural limitations of the one-adult unit, noted at the beginning of this section, obviously make it less likely to be in a position to supply one earner, let alone two. Full-time work may increasingly fail to guarantee freedom from poverty for families in our society, but non-work is clearly more likely to mean low income and/or welfare dependency.

The effect of lone parenthood on the maintenance and extension of poverty and dependency, may be compounded by intergenerational effects. As these characteristics become circular, the children are more likely to be poor, or poor lone parents, than those from intact families who have suffered poverty spells. Thus the children of lone parents are disadvantaged in ways that impair their future and the futures of their children. Over time, family structure may make a disproportionate contribution to persistent and cumulative poverty and welfare dependency, and the evidence is that such negative effects are growing.

Low levels of expenditure on children may derive from other causes than the poverty of lone mothers. Stepfathers and boyfriends are less likely to spend on non-genetic children, particularly if they have no legal tie to their consorts' offspring. There is also less parental time, effort and investment from extended kin. Parental attitudes may be less altruistic and the children more likely to be abandoned or institutionalised.[50] The third British longitudinal study of child development, the Child Health and Education Study, showed how illegitimacy was more likely to result in a child going to live in a foster home, with grandparents, or eventually being adopted.[51]

As this can produce disadvantages in future labour markets, so non-marital fertility may produce a negative effect on overall incomes if it transmits low human capital over generations and increases dependence upon public institutions. These phenomena are not limited to Anglo-Saxon democracies. In the old Soviet Union:

> ... the semi-serf intergenerational underclass of the so-called 'limited people' (rural immigrant workers without permanent residence rights) and their children (many of whom are out-of-wedlock and placed in orphanages) constituted about 15 per cent of the Soviet urban population. The production of children became an instrument for single mothers for claiming the most precious Soviet asset, public housing, and for establishing permanent urban residence. By some official Soviet estimates, this new Soviet underclass had a 78 per cent rate of intergenerational immobility.[52]

In the USA Sara McLanahan found that family welfare history significantly related to daughters' welfare dependency. The longer the family is on welfare (receiving at least 50 per cent of its income this way), the more likely will daughters become recipients.[53] Work is not just a matter of availability, but of the kind of information, association and commitment promoted by parents' present and past employment. Since the couple household is an economic unit and social group in which one parent cares for the children while the other specialises in paid work, it means that the whole unit is attached to the labour market. With a lone parent on public assistance, the children grow up in an environment where no-one is working, and they are mainly or wholly dependent upon outside sources of support. While they are familiar with the welfare system as the provider of first resort, there is no working role model which provides attachment to work and acquaintance with on-the-job behaviour. There is also a lack of the kind of informal contacts or search skills that might be helpful in job finding, particularly for boys, which male relatives often supply. Thus, while children may escape the welfare dependency of their parent, many more than in the general population are also captured by it.

The importance of example and connections is illustrated by the comparison made by the American Bureau of Economic Research of minority youths who were able to find work with those who did not.[54] It found a significant relationship, not only between aspirations and 'right' attitudes, but whether other family members were on public assistance or unemployed. Unemployed British 16-19 year-olds picked up by the General Household Survey were three times more likely to live in a family with another unemployed member, and figures for Youth Training Scheme 'non-participants' show two-thirds as living in households with at least one other unemployed adult.[55] The ability to respond to training opportunities depends very much on whether the young person has a 'conventional home', has parents who are unemployed or on a low income, and on whether their ideas about growing up are tied to getting and succeeding in work. Unemployment rates are considerably higher for children living in a lone-parent household and, where the female head is also unemployed, they are three times more likely to be unemployed than those with couples—with no declines in their rate of joblessness over time.

The adolescent's disadvantage may also be compounded by neighbourhood effects. The chances of dropping out of school or having a baby out of wedlock rise sharply once poverty or dependency levels escalate above a critical threshold—even with family background taken into account.

Being only one adult, the lone parent can find herself caught between the rock and the proverbial hard place. If she becomes

a 'working model' she cannot, of course, care for her children at
the same time and full-time maternal employment has a
worrying connection with poorer intellectual development, mainly
of boys.[56]

The children of lone parents may not fare so well economically
compared to those of couples, irrespective of the financial
position of their mother, because lone parenthood means reduced
social resources for childrearing. The British National Child
Development Study found that 16-year-olds who came, not just
from low-income or large families, but had lone parents, were far
more likely to leave school both early and unprepared for
employment.[57] Children from non-intact families are also far
more likely to leave home before the age of 19, because of the
expectation that they will set up on their own at an early
opportunity. Step-parents and boyfriends are also highly motivated to push their partner's children towards premature
independence. This early termination of parental responsibilities
persists despite controls for economic circumstances, whether in
terms of education, occupation or receipt of public assistance.[58]

If a child experiences divorce, the evidence now points to
adverse effects in terms of health, behaviour and economic status
up to 30 years later. As young men of 18 and 21, those from
the British 1946 cohort study whose parents had divorced were
three times more likely to be unemployed than the offspring of
intact families. Their earning capacity was generally impaired at
26, with twice the expected proportion at age 36 in the lowest
income bracket after controls for social class of origin. A middle
class child was half as likely to go to university and the same
applied to a working class child's likelihood of passing examina-
tions.[59] Men with fathers in non-manual occupations whose
parents were divorced by the time that they were 16 years were
more likely at 23 to be in unskilled manual occupations than
those whose parents had stayed together or had been widowed.
They were even more likely to be in unskilled occupations than
those from intact families whose fathers had been manual
workers. Women are also affected. When Kuh and Maclean
considered the relationship between family disruption, mothers'
education and educational qualification at 26 years, they found
that women who had been through their parents' separation or
divorce were significantly less likely to have any educational
qualifications.[60]

But then all studies which have examined the impact of divorce on children have found that school performance is adversely affected and that they have greater difficulties in reaching educational and occupational goals. The first major report of the National Child Development Study, based on a national sample of children born in March 1958, graded 49 per cent of illegitimate children as poor readers at 7 compared to 28 per cent of those with fathers. Moreover, after eliminating the effects of class and other factors, the children without fathers were found to have an 'arithmetic age' of five months younger.[61]

Greater acceptance of lone parenthood with time has not reduced or eliminated such findings. American data from the National Health Interview Survey on Child Health in 1988 showed how—even after adjustment for all other economic, social and demographic variables—family structure was strongly related to academic performance. The percentage of children having to repeat a grade in school was 21 per cent for children of divorced mothers and 30 per cent for those with never married mothers, compared with 12 per cent of children living in intact families. Children from disrupted marriages were more than twice as likely than those living with both biological parents to have been expelled or suspended; while those with a never married mother were more than three times as likely to have had this experience. Children who did not live with both biological parents were up to twice as likely to have been the subject of a parent-teacher conference than those who did.[62]

In parallel, the National Survey of Children showed how children of divorced parents were consistently more likely to enter special classes and do less well academically.[63] But, perhaps the most comprehensive and detailed study of the effect of living in a lone-parent family on educational attainment was carried out in the USA and used matched mother/child pairs from the National Longitudinal Survey of Labour Market Experience (which followed more than 2,500 children into adulthood) for precise measures of the age and length of time children spent with one parent. The longer the time spent with a lone parent, the greater the reduction in educational attainment, with the largest negative impact on men and during the pre-school years. Controlling for income did not noticeably reduce the magnitude of the effect.[64]

The downward mobility of the children of divorce compared to the parental generation was demonstrated in Judith Wallerstein's and Sandra Blakeslee's pioneering study. Here, 60 per cent of their mainly middle class sample were on a falling educational course compared to their fathers ten years after the divorce (or 45 per cent compared to their mothers).[65] Looking at ten years of data from the Panel Study of Income Dynamics (PSID) (comprising 15,000 families selected in 1968 who have been interviewed annually), Sara McLanahan showed how, regardless of parents' race, education, income or residence, living in a mother-only family reduces the likelihood of completing high school.[66] Virtually identical results were obtained from the 1980 census and from 12,000 children from the High School and Beyond Survey, whose fortunes were mapped out over the 1980s. The numbers were even higher for those children, like those in poverty areas of big cities, who already had a risk of dropping out of school. As they are also increased if the mother left school early, such "results bode ill for future generations born to single teenage mothers who leave school to care for the child".[67]

Understandably, these educational deficits can all make a significant contribution to the likelihood of poverty in later life. American researchers, using the PSID for samples of men born in different years to find out which variables were useful to predict their later income, found future earnings depressed by father absence, especially with the mother also at work. Furthermore, divorced men showed a 20 per cent drop in income and divorced women a 30 per cent drop, compared with an income gain of 20 per cent for married couples.[68]

While parental absence puts more children on a downward course than would otherwise be the case, so, by the same token, less children are removed from disadvantage, with offenders often coming from generally deprived backgrounds. Little publicised British research from the National Child Development Study showed how the "quite remarkable" difference in family situations between children who had done well by age 23, particularly educationally, despite the worst backgrounds in terms of income and housing, was associated with the fact that almost all had stayed with two original parents. Only a half of the comparison group were in this situation. The researchers had predicted the opposite, or that the lone-parent children would do better. This was because, to even qualify for inclusion as severely disadvantaged, two-parent families also had to have five or more children.[69] The results may have been partly explicable in terms of the father's interest and involvement. After all, other material from the National Child Development Study showed a close relationship between children's educational attainment and fathers' interest in intact families generally.[70] However, this study also pointed to the operation of obscure second order effects when a father is present at home, which also seem to be present elsewhere, such as in studies of supervision or reception into care (see Chapter 5).

The Effect on Family Formation

The long-term consequences of parental divorce and upbringing by a lone parent mean that children can be predisposed to repeat patterns of marital disruption and single motherhood in their own lives. This effect on future family formation has been identified as the strongest and probably most important outcome. The evidence suggests a dynamic that will progressively weaken the prevalence of unbroken nuclear families and, in exposing more children to circumstances likely to have other negative consequences for their development, successively undermines the life chances of future generations.

From the PSID sample, Sara McLanahan calculated that exposure to lone parenthood in adolescence increases the rate of becoming a single mother by about 150 percentage points for whites and 90 points for blacks.[71] Data from the National Survey of Family Growth (involving 7,969 women aged 15-44 years), found that women who spent time with a lone parent because of marital disruption or single motherhood, were 111 per cent more likely to have teenage births, 164 per cent more likely to have pre-marital births and 92 per cent more likely to have failed marriages than daughters who grew up in two-parent homes.[72] Other work has shown that daughters of divorced parents are more likely to be divorced themselves, and that adolescent daughters of lone parents are more likely to be sexually active. In Britain Kathleen Kiernan found that young women whose parents' marriages had broken down by the time they were 16 were more likely to cohabit in their teens, to have a child by 20, and to have extra-marital births. These findings were not altered by the introduction of background controls.[73] It is likely that parental role models, together with lack of parental input and supervision, are major factors determining children's future family behaviour.[74]

This means that it is not only the parent's receipt of public assistance which is a significant determining factor for whether the daughters become welfare mothers. Simply having a lone mother increases the likelihood (by 10 per cent for whites and 22 per cent for blacks in American samples), irrespective of income.[75]

Those daughters of divorced parents who do marry also have a far greater chance of having their own marriages break up. For sons, the probability of marriage may be lower in the first place. Divorce can be the first link in a chain of disadvantage, portending educational failure, early termination of training and poor health. Young men from the earliest British cohort study (1946) whose parents had divorced also experienced more chronic illness and a three- to five-fold incidence of mental illness compared with those from intact families. As their poorer prospects make them insecure and irregular workers at the lower end of the job market, this sabotages their chances of both acquiring or retaining mates. As they are far more likely to be single this, in turn, increased their chance not only of being unemployed, but of dropping out of the workforce entirely. Hence Mavis Maclean and M.E.J. Wadsworth found that not only were proportionally more men from divorced homes unemployed and seeking work, but they were unemployed and not seeking work by their mid-30s, both as a matter of choice and as a result of mental and physical disability.[76]

This chapter has explored some of the relationships between lone parenthood and the origins and perpetuation of poverty. The next question is, how do we account for lone parenthood?

Money and Marriage

Summary: *Traditionally those unable to marry did not have children, but modern welfare makes extra-marital childbearing both possible and attractive. The majority of the population continues to see the role of the husband and father as that of breadwinner, but as employment trends have made it increasingly difficult for men to earn enough to support a family, so many women (and men) have become reluctant to marry at all. Cohabitation has begun to replace marriage in low-income communities. As changes in the labour market have reduced the number of full-time jobs for men and increased part-time and women's employment, many men have become unviable as mates. These disruptive trends in the labour market have been compounded by tax policies which make it increasingly difficult for a working man to support a family. Fatherhood makes men more willing to work in the labour force, but motherhood has the opposite effect on women. Programmes to entice lone mothers into the workforce must therefore rely on very large incentives, and may be impractical. Lone mothers are unlikely to be employed and unlikely to marry or remarry, as long as they are supported by adequate welfare. Many lone mothers are of lower than average intelligence, so the jobs open to them would be low paid. The combination of the destabilisation of male earnings with expanded welfare programmes has been destructive of marriage, particularly amongst the poor. A woman may be no worse off, or even better off, without the father of her children. The increase in the resources made available to lone parents coupled with the confiscation of resources from families has resulted in rising numbers of sterile marriages, as many married couples feel they are unable to afford to have any children at all.*

Perverse Incentives

W ELFARE critics allege that benefits for lone mothers discourage providers from remaining as the family support and their availability militates against the formation of the family in the first place. Women are encouraged not to marry a poor prospect and not to stay in marriage.[1] This sets up a circular process: men do not strive to be good providers and women do not expect it or put pressure on the man to behave responsibly. A licence to earn while on welfare is not just an incentive to work for those women who are already recipients, but also provides "a much stronger incentive for women who were not on welfare to get on it and then become trapped in it". The net effect is to raise the value of being eligible for welfare and thereby, "via a classic market response, increase the supply of eligible women".[2] There is, as *The Times* editorialised on 10 November 1993, a very straightforward "statistical fact: the sudden enormous increase in never-married mothers coincided with changes in the social welfare structure which rewarded that group preferentially over married couples".

Many of those who have been out to break the family see the process the same way. In *Splitting Up: Single Parent Liberation*, Catherine Itzin mused on how single parenthood as a "properly serviced status", would acquire "a new and possibly even desirable status in society". Made more economically attractive "single parent families... would threaten the existing social structure".[3] Fran Bennett, as Director of the Child Poverty Action Group, agreed that an income as of right for women, and lone mothers in particular, might tempt them out of the nuclear family set up. Through these means it should be possible to "undermine the different family responsibilities of both sexes" so that "the women might no longer feel dependent on the men, and the men might no longer want to provide for their wives and children".[4] While feminist researchers are loathe to suggest that lone mothers may not be the worst situated or provided for section of the community, they often acknowledge that many already feel better or no worse off than in marriage:

> The high divorce rate ... indicates that economically dependent women often prefer the dependence on and dominance of the state as the 'supreme father'—the structural impersonal patriarchy—to the personal dominance of their husbands, the children's father. The state acting as a substitute parent lessens a woman's dependence on her husband ... and consequently makes women as mothers more independent.[5]

Profit or Loss?

Certainly, outcomes may be seen as the result of the respective attractions to be found in and outside a relationship and the barriers to their realisation.[6] The considerations of men and women about entering a relationship are strongly affected by the relative gains each would experience by moving from single to couple status, just as the degree of dependence of each party on the relationship depends on the relative costs that each would experience should it end. G. Becker in his *Treatise on the Family* characterises the family-formation process as being governed by a continuous search in which men and women evaluate their relative contribution and gain, and will form families to the extent that they are reasonably satisfied with their net balance.[7]

There are rewards to marriage associated with income and ownership, family status, mutual similarity, affection, companionship and sexual enjoyment. Competing with these are the attractions of independence, alternative partners and sources of economic support. The barriers to ending a marriage relate to financial expenses, religious constraints, obligations to the marital bond, the pressures from kin, community or other primary groups and the ties and responsibilities towards dependent children.[8] Variables important at some points in time, may not be relevant at others. Here, the private lives of spouses are never separable from the surrounding social and economic environment, and it is these as much as matters internal to relationships that will influence the formation and dissolution of marriages.

So, as economists like John Ermisch agree, if welfare payments in cash and kind for lone mothers raise the welfare available outside the married state enough, any economic reasons for forming a conjugal household disappear.[9] Obviously, relative attractions are crucial to an incentives or choice model and involve both the comparative treatment of lone and married parents by the means-tested welfare system and the general tax and benefit structure. It is not simply that as people:

> ... see that their relatives can get reasonable provisions from the public purse, they may, as tax-payers (if comfortably off themselves) or as needy citizens themselves (if poor), decide to reduce the level of support to their own family. A point will arrive when many people come to see the state rather than the family as the place of first resort when in need.[10]

This is also likely to be facilitated if, at the same time, there is little or no general recognition or allowance made for those supporting dependants, and these are treated no more favourably, or even less so, than those without dependants. And, since we are concerned with what prospective and actual husbands have to offer as well as what welfare is paying, so the earnings of men, before as after taxation, will play a role in the attractiveness of marriage compared with going solo. Factors like the ease or difficulty of finding a spouse with stable employment, or rising or falling levels of male earnings, are bound to confound predictions based on welfare alone. These might be expected to exert an independent effect on marriage and birth patterns even in the absence of public assistance for unsupported mothers.

Too narrow a focus on lone mothers themselves leads us to neglect what is going on with men as the missing husbands and fathers; just as a preoccupation with lone-parent poverty leads us away from how families generally are faring. The fortunes of families may be vital to understanding present family trends. We have to ask as much why people do not form or stay in families, as why women become lone parents. As the mother and child unit is now promoted as a different or alternative 'family form', rather than seen in terms of the fragmentation of the family, this can suggest that we are dealing with two distinct populations. But a major reason why the proportion of out-of-wedlock births has assumed such dimensions is, after all, because there is less marriage and fewer and fewer babies are being born to married women. Changes in family structure reflect marriage and children postponed or forgone, as much or more than an upsurge in births to single women. Thus, we must address the factors which are influencing women to have fewer children within marriage as much as those which are leading women to have babies outside.

However, it has always to be borne in mind that, while economic circumstances may lead people to forgo marriage and desert families and may be sufficient to induce non-marriage and childlessness, this may be insufficient for non-marital childbearing. After all, the traditional pattern has been childlessness in marriage and celibacy outside on the part of the long-term poor or hard pressed. Non-marital fertility declined along with marital fertility during the Great Depression. Thus, need joblessness and lack of permanent income alone (without differential welfare payments) generate single motherhood? If not, then changes in institutional arrangements, as well as economic opportunities, are needed to explain the high modern rates of out-of-wedlock births.[11]

In turn, while income from welfare may be evaluated in comparison with other income opportunities, we must not assume that non-marital fertility is the 'first-best choice' of the people involved. An abiding preference has been for marriage, work and the success of one's children—subject to having the means. The degree to which welfare influences people to opt for the 'second best' choice, or single motherhood, depends on the extent to which alternative opportunities are lacking. By the same token, increases in opportunities outside the public assistance system will lead to the abandonment of lower rated choices.

Being the Breadwinner: A Demand Men Cannot Meet?

Despite the claims of establishment feminists that "The bread-winner role is, to an increasing extent, not socially relevant as mothers are also contributing to the financial existence of the family",[12] husbands were still providing an average of 87.8 per cent of the income in households with one earner and dependent children in 1989, and 69 per cent where there were two earners.

What is more, over three-quarters of husbands and wives still define the male parenting role as including being the main provider and see breadwinning as the anchor of a father's role.[13] Because people do not support the view that paid employment is the sole prerogative of the breadwinner, or deny that women have a right to seek employment, is no rejection of the idea that men must be the mainstays of families. In Bill Jordon and colleagues' study of low-income households, men's decision making was within a moral framework of how men should work and provide for families.[14] Similarly, in Elaine Kempson and colleagues' *Hard Times?*, men and women overwhelmingly saw the responsibility of being the main wage earner as a man's responsibility, even if the wives worked.[15] Considerations such as the incentive and disincentive effects of wages, benefits and taxation, were framed in reference to the way that the labour market and the tax and benefit systems shaped and constrained their efforts to fulfill their primary roles. Success requires 'good' labour decisions, and men try to present themselves as living up to its moral requirements.

Delivering income to a family means that a man's earnings are seen as a 'family wage', even when rates of pay and conditions of employment do not correspond with the notion of a predictable and large enough income to meet household needs. As in one study of youth unemployment, young men's aspirations about marrying were tied up with those for sufficient resources "for homes of their own, children, cars and a little money to fall back on". Where this was not achievable, they were hostile to the notion of marriage.[16] A 'good' job is still largely inseparable for men from one which will support a family adequately, or go a long way towards this end. Where they lack this, they often avoid enduring relationships with women. In turn, there must be some ability to predict the future in terms of employment and earnings, otherwise it becomes difficult to make the kind of long-term plans involved in family building and it becomes desirable to be open-ended, or non-committal. Individual level data for American males born between 1907 and 1953 show how employed men are significantly more likely to marry than unemployed men, who abandon the marriage market during periods of high unemployment.[17] Men's marital fortunes are not just owed to personal experience, but to all manner of wider, political, economic and social factors, like government expenditure on higher education, the nature of labour markets and military obligations, as these will affect perceptions of the costs and benefits of marriage.

Without a 'decent' job, men are also undesirable spouses and marriage patterns are consistent with the assumption that women are particularly likely to consider marriage when a prospective husband earns more than some minimum threshold. This seems relatively resistant to change in the face of fluctuating labour market prospects. Certainly the evidence indicates that the overall fall in wages of black American men since the 1960s has not led to women scaling down their expectations. Hence, the far smaller numbers of men marrying are those who have been fortunate enough still to have incomes close to the level of the 1960s in the 1980s.[18]

A long line of demographic and ethnographic research links male employment to family formation and marital stability, as part of a consistently demonstrable and direct relationship between the timing of marriage and economic conditions. The more encouraging the latter, the earlier and more commonly will people marry. Investigation of poverty in Tudor and Stuart England shows how sudden upward surges in bastardy were largely the result of disrupted betrothals when economic downturns limited marriage opportunities for the poor.[19] Robert D. Mare and Christopher Winship's analysis from American census data between 1940 and 1980, as well as population surveys for 1985-7, showed both how increases in the expected probability of employment raised the likelihood of marriage. For example, a $100 increase in weekly earnings raised the odds of marriage for young men by about 30 per cent (or 20 per cent for those aged 30-39).[20]

William Julius Wilson and Kathryn M. Neckerman first showed long-term decline in the MMPI (Marriageable Male Pool Index) in American black communities, where parallel trends in employment and marriage both fell gradually in the 1960s then rapidly in the 1970s and 1980s, and suggested that joblessness was a major underlying factor in the growth of female headed households. Extraordinarily, while there were about seven employed black males to 10 adult women in Northern inner cities in the 1950s, this plummeted to around two men for every 10 women in some areas, so that "no other group has experienced such a rapid and near total depletion of the pool of marriageable men".[21] Subsequent work supports their contention that a foremost identifiable or quantifiable reason for the contraction of two-parent families is that men cannot afford marriage. Not only is male unemployment the strongest predictor of the total of female headed households anywhere in America but, as in Robert J. Sampson's comprehensive analysis, income and occupational status are inversely related to marital instability and illegitimacy.[22] Rates of family disruption and single parenthood are higher for areas where there is not only a higher mean welfare payment, but the pool of employed males is low and there is a low per-capita income. Mediated by the resulting family disruption, unemployment and poverty are associated with high levels of criminality and violence. If this puts more men in prison or otherwise under the control of the policing and penal system, the pool of marriageable males is further reduced: as it is by greater mortality among single men.

The larger the proportion of people out of work and the larger the proportion in unskilled or semi-skilled jobs, so the higher the illegitimacy ratio. British municipal districts with high concentrations of household heads in class I (professional and managerial), had low illegitimacy ratios in the late 1980s, while nearly half the births might be out of wedlock in those with largely unskilled populations.[23]

Those most vulnerable to the vicissitudes of the economy are also likely to avoid marriage in favour of casual and conditional relationships, where they can keep their options open in the face of uncertain economic prospects. A national survey of Australians aged between 18 and 34 found that cohabitation was usually a temporary arrangement until couples felt financially secure enough to marry. Cohabiting unions have high failure rates, because financial insecurity militates against personal stability.

It is clear that a large majority of British cohabiting mothers are in disadvantaged circumstances. Over half had household incomes in the lowest ranges (18 per cent of cohabiting couples with children had net incomes of less than £6,000 in 1992, compared with 6 per cent of women who married before having children); a quarter lived in households where nobody was employed and one-fifth had a partner who had been unemployed for over two years.[24] Similar results were obtained from General Household Survey data of 1989. Cohabitating couples with children were the poorest group, and 23 per cent had gross weekly incomes of less than £100 compared to six per cent of married parents. The picture has often been distorted by the presence of upper middle class dual career and childless couples who are prominent as trend setters in the women's press and media generally. As expected, almost 50 per cent of childless cohabiting or married couples had weekly incomes over £400, and 25 per cent of childless cohabitees had incomes over £500 compared to 10 per cent of cohabitees and 12 per cent of the married with children.[25] For cohabiting parents the passage into marriage is associated with financial resources or labour market advantage, and tends to happen as people acquire assets such as houses, savings and pensions.

If the benefits of a division of labour will also tend to make marriage more attractive, then factors which reduce specialisation at home, such as when both partners are employed for similar hours at similar rates, also increase the risk that the household will dissolve by reducing the gains from co-operation. (By the same token, the decline in men's earnings in relation to women's reduces the economic advantages of marriage for women and makes staying single more attractive to start with.) Even as there has been a rapid increase in dual earner families, marriages where the husband is the main provider are still less likely to break up compared with those where both partners are unemployed, employed full-time or there is role reversal.[26] It is not only difficult for two fully employed parents to co-operate effectively and cover all aspects of the parental role between them, but these also tend to be circumstances of great pressure, overload, and constant fatigue, with reports of high levels of conflict and stress.[27] Although balancing job and family demands is often extremely difficult for parents of older children, they are most incompatible in the early years. If there are more reasons for dissatisfaction and less advantages in staying together, then divorce will become more likely. John Ermisch's analysis of data from the British Women and Employment survey showed how mothers who had been employed 80 per cent of the time since giving birth had roughly double the probability of divorce as mothers who did not work.[28]

Individual level studies of family dissolution, analyses of trends in separation and divorce over time, as well as census, or cross-sectional, data, all show a strong connection between income and divorce.[29] This is not evenly distributed among the various age and economic groups, even if its increase has been pervasive with regard to social and economic level. The higher the husband's earnings the less likely are couples to part. The close correlation between low socio-economic status and increased marital dissolution means that it is the marriages of the manual working classes and the unemployed that are most likely to be dissolved. While it is among the less skilled that we find a concentration of indicators of divorce, such as young age at marriage, premarital pregnancy, housing difficulties, lack of combined assets, and so forth, low income is in the lead. The association between low divorce proneness and high husband education tends to disappear once income level is considered, as do occupational differences. Even research on the survival rates of marriages after application for divorce has shown an inverse relationship between the fate of the application and the husband's income.[30]

Job insecurity at marriage is associated with dissolution. The weak economic position of the young father provides a strong link between pre-marital pregnancy and the high breakdown rates of subsequent marriages.[31] Of course, the couple's courtship and adjustment process is disrupted and truncated by premature parental responsibilities as, at the same time, there is limited wage-earning capacity when the presence of a child demands more income. While personal incompatibility was most often reported as the major reason why marriages broke down in one study, more than one out of every four wives explicitly attributed the failure of the marriage to the husband's inability to support the family. Young fathers who were able to improve their economic position during the course of this investigation of premarital pregnancy and marital dissolution had noticeably higher marital stability.

But at any point in a marriage, joblessness substantially raises the chance of divorce. An analysis by John Haskey of men who divorced in 1979 found that the rate among the unemployed was higher than for any other British class or group apart from the armed forces, while L. Lampard found that in British cities in the 1980s the husband's unemployment was associated with a 70 per cent increase in the risk of marital breakdown the next year.[32]

The father's position in the family is strongly related to his external position, so that he is often unwelcome at home when he fails to achieve the occupational status and security necessary to sustain a reasonable standard of living or, at least, cover basic costs. And, of course, an increase in men in the family building stage with insufficient resources to support a family above poverty level, if at all, also contributes to that familiar historical pattern, where wives (and children) bring in income. But these are the circumstances in which wives are not only more likely to work, but to resent it. Parents who have to take small children to care based outside the home, or operate alternative shifts, where the wife leaves for work as the father comes home, suffer the greatest stress, and are deprived of time together in which to maintain a common perspective. Barbara Thornes and Jean Collard found that the duration of marriages of wives who worked because they needed the money was much shorter than for those who did not work, or did so from personal choice for an outside interest.[33]

The lower class man may command less marital loyalty, primarily because he offers less long-term security. It is not only that his economic contribution may be unacceptably low but also that the prospects for improvement in the future are poor or non-existent. In other words, he is a poor investment.[34]

At the bottom of the class ladder, the likelihood of divorce or separation is higher than the chances of remarriage. Only a small percentage of American lone mothers will marry off welfare, although this has been the leading way in which exits are made. One study showed how 'marrying out' occurred for only 13 per cent of lone parents on public assistance over a three-year period.[35] Conversely, while men in high status groups have a below-average propensity to be divorced, they also have an above-average likelihood of remarriage if they do divorce.

The Two-Way Process

Getting married and being in work are closely connected for men, so that not working is a strong predictor of not being married. If one of two props breaks, the other does not hold for long. If 'good' jobs that pay enough to support a family decline, lower class young men respond by postponing marriage, but taking poorly paid, short-term jobs. But as they age, those who do not find steady jobs become reluctant to take any work and, lacking the spur of actual or prospective marriage, drop out of the workforce.[36] In turn, the stability of the father's income is a necessary condition for the stability of fatherhood. Danile Bertaux and Catherine Delcroix's interviews with men on French streets led them to the "inescapable conclusion" that a man cannot stay a father without an income of his own, no matter what its origins or nature:

> ... for adult men who had been cornered into uninteresting, dead end jobs, the courage needed to get up every morning and go to work fed upon the necessity to make a living not for oneself (it would perhaps not be worth it), but for one's loved ones. It was out of duty toward one's children that men worked; but if the children were removed, taking away the meaning of duty with them, then the meaning of work was also lost.
>
> Conversely, losing one's job makes it harder to remain a father. The precariousness of a job corrodes the status ... that is, those men who do have jobs, but ones which come and go, lack one of the attributes that make a father out of a man.[37]

Unviable Mates?

If the rates of single parenthood rise where there is high unemployment and low wages, then they are also likely to rise over time not only where a smaller percentage of men hold jobs, or their earnings are lowered, but also when future prospects are unpredictable and precarious. This is what is happening as we experience levels of economic insecurity unprecedented since the early industrial revolution. The decreasing ability of men to make sufficient and stable provision for families has probably played a pivotal role in generating high rates of non-marriage, family breakdown and a rising proportion of children without fathers on both sides of the Atlantic. The growth, not merely of unemployment, but of jobs which neither pay much nor survive very long, and a tax system progressively disinclined to recognise family responsibilities, have produced a momentous change in the marital as well as the economic opportunities of populations. The drop in marriage rates cannot be explained simply by falling earnings and employment; it is also related to general apprehension about family life, where economic uncertainty is part of an insecure climate of expectations.

The timing, spacing and frequency of births all affect marital stability insofar as they create economic stress. As pressures on couples intensify, the circumstances are growing in which a birth is economically 'unwise' and, therefore, inauspicious for the marital relationship.

While equality activists rage at "dominant ideologies" that "define the 'good' father and the 'good' worker in ways that sustain present patterns of male employment",[38] the irony is that the amount of support, if any, that men, especially at younger ages, are able to offer families, has been drastically reduced by momentous changes in labour markets and taxation. However these changes might be appraised on other criteria, they now foster whole communities in which it is very difficult to establish and maintain families, with almost insuperable obstacles to family formation at the bottom of the socio-economic ladder.

Men's jobs traditionally dominated economies, but the workforce representation of men has shrunk enormously in the last two decades and at an accelerating pace. Jobs predominantly held by men are a declining segment of the economy and it is male unemployment that stays high even when demand for labour picks up. Rapid deindustrialisation has ended massive numbers of jobs in shipbuilding, iron and steel works, motor manufacture, dock work, and other heavy and extractive industries. These traditionally provided whole communities with the livelihoods that enabled each generation of working men to support a home by paying a 'living wage', understood as an income sufficient to support a wife and children at a modest standard of comfort.

The new de-regularised labour market is one where long-term security of tenure has given way to short-term and 're-negotiable' agreements at all levels, in public services, banking and finance, as much as in industry. Public employers have been compelled to contract out to the lowest tenderers with their pools of self-employed labour. Nobody, even in farming, can expect 'jobs for life', and specialists and professionals have also become disposable labour to be 'plugged in' as required.

This means that the integration of employment with family responsibilities vanishes for white collar and professional staffs as it has done for manual workers. Instead of consolidating his position and rising up the hierarchy with incremental increases in earnings as his family expenses grow, a man approaching mid-life might as much expect to be dismissed, or to look in vain for another assignment as his contract expires. It is not simply that he can be replaced by a younger, cheaper worker. Also reflected is the movement sweeping through public organisations to clear out the older men and promote women. The trend to horizontal, business organisation with short career ladders, serves both market flexibility, and the desire of the equal rights movement to undermine the way in which couples often focus on building up the husband's job in the childrearing years. As the equality movement gained momentum in the 1980s the dismantling of barriers became positive recruitment, or 'affirmative action' to ensure that women were not 'under-represented'. The traditional reluctance to threaten the jobs of established workers was based on the rationale that many supported wives and children, but now there are no qualms about the impoverishment of the breadwinner's family. On the contrary, the loss of his job means one woman can step into his position while another at home is propelled onto the labour market.

While reflecting the family's mounting insecurity, the rise of the working mother, anxious to keep her employment to a minimum necessary to meet basic commitments, has helped companies to 're-structure' with contingent workers. The expansion of part-time work accounted for virtually all the new jobs created in Britain in the 1980s (and, in turn, accounts for the expansion of the female labour force). The move towards a seven-day trading week is calculated to convert more than half a million retail jobs from full- to part-time, or ones which customarily provided additional, rather than basic, family income. Even when fewer people are recorded as unemployed, full-time jobs continue to drop (near four lost for men to every one for women in the 1990s recession). Men began to move into part-time jobs, usually associated with married women, so that over this time there has been an overall growth of 25 per cent in male part-timers, as full-time jobs for men were down by 1.4 million.[39]

As there have been policy-making departures away from strategies to maintain full employment and a high wage economy, unemployment also became a tool of anti-inflationary policy. Full employment was once basic to government programmes of family support, preceding and enshrined in the Beveridge package of the early 1940s. Micro-policies related to job security and tenure, working conditions, wages, while macro-employment policies dealt with matters like investment, public works and foreign-exchange management. These were tied to direct pro-family measures such as tax relief, family allowances, services for children, housing subsidies, controls on rents and interest rates.

The Most Vulnerable

Between 1960 and 1990, Britain lost more than 3 million relatively well paid, full-time jobs for semi- or unskilled male factory workers. This is particularly significant since these once provided a major entry point into the world of work for youngsters without the skills or paper qualifications for white- collar work. Technology has also taken its toll of lower-grade office work and labour-intensive shops and stores have declined. In turn, wage developments have had their sharpest impact on younger workers, of whom a rising proportion earn less than the Council of Europe's decency threshold.[40]

While the statistics also show family or child poverty to be growing in the 1970s, then rising faster in the 1980s, another trend also becomes apparent, involving increasing numbers of single (childless)—and, it seems, overwhelmingly young—people in the poorest income groups. The numbers on Income Support have more or less trebled since 1979 and those with net resources below this level (or with average resources of only 57 per cent of Income Support) have more than doubled (from

570,000 in 1979 to 1,330,000 in 1989). While an estimated two-thirds are in multiple households and may be receiving some support from relatives or friends, it might be said that, should they be male, hopes of becoming husbands are small. Single, full-time workers with resources within 140 per cent of Income Support rose from 130,000 to 270,000 between 1979 and 1989.[41]

America has been used to falling male wage rates for all but the very highly qualified since the mid-1970s. While a middle-income man turning 40 years-old in 1963 saw his real income rise 30 per cent by the time he turned 50 years-old, his 1973 counterpart faced a 14 per cent drop in the next ten years and ended up earning less than his father.

It is possible that family behaviour provides a very sensitive barometer, or early indicator, of economic dislocations, which will generally strike the weakest first. Trends towards single motherhood, divorce and casual associations have been led by segments of the population most vulnerable to adverse economic developments. Caught in a vicious spiral, communities with high levels of joblessness, concentrations of the poor, and pronounced family disruption, also undergo a weakening of formal and voluntary organisations which play crucial roles in linking youth to wider social institutions and in fostering desired principles and values. This accelerates the growth of dependence on public assistance and leads to the appellation of 'underclass'.

In 1965, Daniel Patrick Moynihan first drew attention to a rise in family breakdown and illegitimacy among American blacks which augured badly for their advancement.[42] At the time he seemed to be describing an inexplicable phenomenon limited to lower class blacks. However, it later became apparent that these communities were being affected by changes in agriculture, industry and migration. As black urbanisation overtook that of whites by 1950, this made blacks extra vulnerable to the impending post-industrial changes that were to transform the opportunity structures of cities.

But what we see here, as everywhere, is the way in which the increase in lone parenthood is tied to the falling fortunes of two-parent families. It is neatly illustrated by the way that the rates of female headed families in 41 American cities are inversely related to the income of intact families, so that one rises as the other falls.[43] This relationship is obscured when two-parent families are represented as well off or advantaged compared to lone parents, which seems to rule out the possibility that the first could be under stresses that are affecting the formation of the second. If it is men with higher incomes who can more easily afford to be married, and better-off families are more likely to stay together, this is bound to lower the average income of lone parents compared to an average for families, even as these suffer downward pressure.

A Basis for Babies

Public assistance for lone mothers was developed to provide an alternative to work for women who lack spousal support from the late 1970s and, as we have seen, this coincided with a considerable rise in welfare dependency in Britain. Australia also saw an enormous upsurge in the numbers dependent upon Supporting Parent Benefit, and a subsequent rapid rate of increase, after the six months qualifying period was removed in 1980. (The numbers rose five-fold in ten years.)[44]

In America, the pattern of growth in the Aid to Families with Dependent Children (AFDC) caseload corresponds closely to the change in the level and availability of the benefit. Between 1963 and 1972 the average real benefit (for a family of four) increased by 35 per cent, with Medicaid, housing, school meals, food stamps and other benefits adding to the welfare package. It may well have looked attractive to women with limited work skills, little education and poor marriage prospects and, in this period, the percentage of female headed families going on the AFDC programme increased from 29 per cent to 63 per cent. June O'Neill has calculated from the records that, for example, a 50 per cent increase in monthly AFDC and Food Stamps will precipitate a 75 per cent increase in both the numbers of women enrolled on the programme and in the number of years spent on AFDC, together with a 43 per cent increase in out-of-wedlock births.[45] The behaviour of young men is also affected through the reduction of employment incentives. There is less pressure to get work because the necessity to support a family is reduced and they might be able to share in the mothers' benefits instead. Between 1963 and 1972, when American AFDC levels and welfare participation rose together, there was also a 50 per cent rise in the number of female headed families. Australia and Britain had much the same experience a decade or so later.

However, there has been less argument over the dependency aspect of means-tested benefits compared with their possible role in family disruption and fragmentation, when they are also targeted on lone mothers. Obviously, providing someone with an income substitute for employment is, by definition, a discouragement to work—and it will be greater the larger the benefit in relation to possible wages. Unsurprisingly, perhaps, 47 per cent of participants in 'Return to Work' programmes run in Britain by the National Council for One Parent Families said they would be worse off at work and 27 per cent complained of the lack of "well-paid jobs".[46]

It seems rational for dependency to be high, and earnings exits low, when women have low earning potential, high work expenses, or high welfare benefits. When earnings exits occurred in America, they were closely linked to qualifications, education, older children and lower welfare benefits, as these vary across the states.[47] As cash benefit levels of AFDC fell in real terms in America in the 1980s, and eligibility criteria were tightened, the welfare caseload stopped rising for the country as a whole. There was some rise in the percentage of lone mothers working, but nothing like the escalation in employed married mothers. But then, a lone parent in Pennsylvania in 1989 earning 50 per cent above minimum rates was still only slightly better off than if she did not work at all and lost her medical protection.

It happens with any group. As disability or invalidity benefits were expanded in America and Britain, a larger proportion of the population registered as disabled. As American public pensions rose in value, so the work participation of men over 64 fell sharply from 47 per cent in 1948 to 16 per cent in 1984. There is also the 'shadow' effect, as those moving towards retirement age are more likely to drop out as well, particularly if there are less calls on income from dependants.

Suitable Work for Mothers

For a father, children provide the impetus to increase employment whenever this might be marginally worthwhile. For mothers work competes with the attraction of being with their children. They may be less sensitive than men to work incentives, so that it takes big enticements or differences between welfare and non-welfare income to move them into the workforce. In America's peak welfare years, not only did more lone mothers drop out of the workforce, but the expansion of the welfare caseload was inflated by those who were allowed to collect AFDC and work at the same time, perhaps by moving into preferred part-time jobs. Welfare mothers could keep the first US$30 of monthly earnings, plus a third of additional earnings, plus work expenses. When this was disallowed in 1981, the drop in the caseload was partly accounted for by the working mothers who moved off benefit (although, as in Britain, it is impossible to calculate the numbers working casually 'on the black', while also collecting public assistance). Thus, it may be easier to shift working lone mothers onto welfare, where this can supplement their wages, than to shift lone mothers on welfare out into the full-time workforce.

With lone parents withdrawing from the workforce in Britain in the 1980s while the number of employed married mothers grew, there may be a greater correspondence between preference and practice in their case. The proportions for married women show the same decline with increasing numbers of children. Eight per cent of lone parents with children under five were working full time in 1990, compared with 14 per cent of married mothers (and 13 to 31 per cent part time). For children aged between five and ten, 20 per cent of lone mothers worked full time compared to 22 per cent of married mothers, with 29 per cent and 48 per cent respectively working part time (changes in benefit rules, allowing full Family Credit to be drawn for part-time work had yet to work through). Both economically inactive lone parents and married mothers insist that they are looking after home and children and are not unemployed.[48]

Women generally prefer not to work when a child is small, and then to work part time with the child at school. British Social Attitudes Survey respondents, when asked to choose which work arrangements they thought best when there was a child under five mostly (76 per cent) opted for the mother at home all the time. (When the question was put a different way in the more recent International Social Attitudes Report, there was two-thirds support for this option.)[49] If money were not the problem, two-thirds of working mothers with small children would be at home and, significantly, this rises to over 80 per cent in lower income groups.[50]

The structure of mothers' employment reflects a resistance to paid work. As more have entered the workforce, there is now a downward trend in average hours. Whereas in 1979, 29.8 per cent of female manual workers worked less than 16 hours a week, by 1990, the figure was 43.7 per cent. Much is made of how mothers, married or not, are desperate to join the full-time workforce. While financial necessity may be driving more there, no evidence suggests that this is what they want. Mothers like to mould paid work around their family responsibilities. The growth of women in better paid, high status employment in Britain, as elsewhere, has largely been a function of the absence of dependent children—if not throughout life, then before and after children have been reared. This considered, when a Department of Social Security Report on Lone Parents and Work reports that most of the lone mothers said they wanted a job one day, it does not mean they are jumping to get out *right now*. Only a quarter were looking for a job to start within a year.[51] Preliminary results from the National Council for One Parent Families' intensive Return to Work Programmes, designed to mobilise and motivate lone parents into taking the first steps into work and build bridges into jobs and training, show that only 13 per cent actually entered employment (projected number 25 per cent), while 40 per cent preferred some sort of further education course (projected number 30 per cent).[52]

Thus, while the claim is that 91 per cent of British lone parents on Income Support say they want to work, only 28 per cent in an important survey in 1991 said now or 'soon' and 63 per cent would rather it be 'later', usually because they wanted to look after their children. Over a third of the 'laters' might have made it 'soon' if childcare were available but, even then, a third emphatically did not want to work.[53] Taking into account those who wished to make changes, either way, now or soon, there would be an overall decline in lone parents on Income Support of 23 per cent. While this might be pushed up by the prospect of easily available childcare, it has to be remembered that those who cite this as an obstacle to returning to work, or an enticement that might make them work 'sooner', are a minority of unoccupied lone parents, or 22 per cent in one study (1980), 37 per cent (with under 5-year-olds) in another (1984) and 26 per cent elsewhere (1991).[54]

Denmark, like Sweden, is one of those 'model' childcare states that has endeavoured to put every mother into the workforce. Here the labour force participation of lone parents is, on the face of it, even higher than that of all mothers at 91 per cent compared to 86 per cent. However, their actual employment is 64 per cent to 82 per cent, owing to their tendency to register as unemployed, even though they are more likely than couples to have only one child and less likely to have a child under 5-years-old. Other figures which include the 'lone' parents who are cohabiting, show a watered down version of the same pattern. Moreover, despite high employment by international standards and hardly any teenage single mothers, about a third of lone parents' disposable income comes from benefits, compared to only 5 per cent in couple families, and 61 per cent from employment, compared to 87 per cent for couples. About a quarter receive public assistance and, of these, four out of ten are dependent for more than five years. Lack of time for their own children is a problem cited by lone parents, as by mothers generally, and the picture is of considerable discontent with long working hours where there are dependent children.[55]

Day care may not be so important to lone parents' employment as its advocates claim. Sceptics like those involved with work projects in America, where less has often been spent than was allocated for childcare, suggest that if mothers really want to work they are often adept at arranging something, usually with relatives or friends. In the mid-1980s, 42 per cent of the childcare provided for working lone parents came from relatives, compared to 28 per cent using organised day care.[56] Many welfare recipients are simply not particularly motivated to resolve childcare problems. They use these as a reason for not co-operating with mandatory work programmes or, if they are exempt because of having very young children, as an acceptable 'excuse' for staying at home.

The work of William L. Parish and colleagues demonstrates how childcare costs are difficult to sustain against a model of attachment to the labour force.[57] Using data from a nationally representative sample of young black and white American mothers, what they found to be important was not non-working kin who could provide childcare, but employed kin who somehow linked the respondents to the labour market. It was this which promoted long-term economic security through work experience. As elsewhere, labour force participation increased as the costs declined (fewer children, older children): economic opportunities increased (more education and lower local unemployment) and income substitutes receded (lesser or no welfare payments). But while the researchers had assumed that the availability of non-employed female kin would provide low-cost childcare, thus lowering the costs of entering the workforce and encouraging workforce participation, the opposite turned out to be the case. Certainly, a third of the working lone mothers turned to kin for help with childcare. But, overall, non-employed kin in the same household depressed employment, while the more employed kin there were, the more likely were lone parents to work. This demonstrated the work-promoting effects of current and past parental and sibling employment, suggesting a strong 'encouraged worker' or 'culture of employment' effect.[58]

In turn, working kin, particularly male kin, often raised the lone mother's living standard by providing substantial cash support when she lived at home. This also depended on these kin themselves being employed and the lone parent not moving away to set up her own welfare-dependent household. The warning is that:

> programs directed solely at mothers ... are no substitute for more general programs designed to raise the employment and income levels of the total community in which these women and their kin are involved.[59]

The fact that mothers want to be with their small children, and the lack of working role models and contacts in communities where welfare dependency is high, are not the only barriers to gainful employment for lone mothers. A perennial panacea in the welfare debate, like the childcare which promises to send mothers rushing into the workforce and up the earnings scale, is the educational and job training to obtain those really 'good jobs'. But experience points to the impotence of such programmes. While American federal and state legislators devised lots of schemes to move lone mothers 'off the welfare rolls and onto payrolls' in the 1980s, they had little success. Indeed, despite years of trying, it has not been possible to raise the wage rates of welfare recipients by more than a tiny amount. The US Department of Labor completed a controlled evaluation of its massive Job Training Partnership Act (JPTA) programme. It found that the wages of female trainees had been raised by 3.4 per cent an hour and the male rate not at all.[60]

One reason for failure might be the low intelligence of many welfare mothers. In America, over half are in the bottom 20 per cent of the population distribution and the average aptitude and achievement scores are significantly below the mean of the lowest occupational classes.[61] In Britain, lone mothers are more likely to fall into the lowest educational and skills groups compared to married women. The gap is likely to grow as unwed, rather than divorced, women make up a greater part of the total of lone parents. An intensive educational and social work programme for 1,408 teenagers in 10 US states has now reported that, after 18 months, those mothers who had joined New Chance were no more likely to be off welfare or in any job than those who had received no services (around 80 per cent were still on welfare). The programme also failed to raise literacy, improve parenting skills, or reduce repeat pregnancies. Despite counselling and contraceptive help, 57 per cent of the women in the programme became pregnant compared with 53 per cent in the control group.[62]

Clearly, the future of any plans to end welfare as we know it must depend upon such results. President Clinton's plan has been for AFDC to be limited to 24 months. If the mother is offered a job, she must take it. If she is still unemployed after the 24 months, she will be offered a publicly subsidised job at the minimum wage. The youngest, and hardest to employ, claimants are to be involved first. Giving childcare to welfare recipients only, and not hard pressed families, might seem to provide a classic incentive to get on welfare for the qualifying 24 months, instead of trying to work your own way from the start. Questions also abound about the size of the necessary public works programme, particularly if welfare mothers cannot be moved easily into the private sector. Moreover, what happens to children when non-working mothers are refused welfare or, alternatively, what is going to be the effect of childcare on children's development, when much of that which is available, particularly for low-income women, is already of a poor, if not a downright, abusive, standard?[63] Experience across the world, as in the former Soviet territories, is that it is counterproductive to push less educated or unskilled mothers into the labour force, particularly considering the high cost and low quality of much substitute care.

But, whatever the number of mothers who turn up for jobs, and however their children fare, this will not improve the prospects for young men and thus for future family formation.

Indeed, even if there is 'rehabilitation' to any degree, will it not further pull down the wage rate by adding to the supply of semi-skilled and unskilled labour? This brings us to perhaps the most important objection to such welfare reforms, that they are the solution to the wrong problem. On every side, from feminists, liberals and the right, it is assumed that the problem is, as Myron Magnet claims, "fundamentally an employment problem of young women".[64] Child development is completely subordinated to the supposed economic interests of their mothers, or rather the equality activists obsession with career outcomes. If children are considered at all, it seems to be assumed that, once the mothers are at work, "Their new independence will kindle in them other qualities needed to make them good mothers and, even beyond that, good citizens". This is bizarre, as getting mothers into the workforce will do nothing, of itself, to improve the nurture, socialisation and success of children being born into fatherless families.

Married to the State?

When people argue about the effects of benefits on divorce, remarriage or out-of-wedlock births, they often take for granted that the gains from marriage are static. However this, as we have seen, is unlikely to be the situation in the real world, where prospects tend to be constantly changing. Moreover, the welfare package includes not only the level of cash benefits, but factors like the ease of getting it, the long-term reliability, and other 'passport' or other associated entitlements. American research suggests that people tend not to respond to any one dimension of welfare in particular, but to their general assessment of the benefits and restrictiveness of the programme in their area.[65] Similarly, much recent British investigation shows how the dependability of benefit income is very important to people's decisions about whether or not to work and, directly or by implication, whether to marry.[66] Then there are matters of familiarity and example, where there is a strong association between having a welfare-dependent birth and the receipt of public assistance by sisters, mothers and other members of the family.[67]

The American evidence has been clear for a long time that welfare levels retard remarriage for divorcees and first marriage for women who have had an out-of-wedlock birth, as well as encouraging girls with babies to set up households apart from their extended families. Irwin Garfinkel and Sarah McLanahan estimate that the increase in welfare benefits accounted for 9 per cent to 14 per cent of the growth in mother-only families between 1960 and 1975, and for possibly 30 per cent of the growth at the bottom of the income distribution, mainly by affecting divorce rates.[68]

However, more recent research like that of C.R. Winegarten suggests that half of the increase in black illegitimacy in recent times can be attributed to welfare effects.[69] For the 1980s researchers like Robert D. Plotnick show the significant effect of differences in the welfare guarantee between states on white and black (but not Hispanic) out-of-wedlock births, whether or not considered in relation to factors like the level of unemployment in local labour markets or real *per capita* income in the state concerned.[70] By this time, it is plausible that the stigma of illegitimacy and other social controls that inhibit out-of-wedlock childbearing had declined relative to earlier years, when they played a stronger role in damping down potential responses to economic incentives. It is consistent with this finding that the effect of welfare on marital status in America also increased from the late 1960s into the 1980s. At this time John Ermisch, using data on 5,320 women gathered in 1980, cautiously estimated that higher welfare benefits and unemployment contributed to an upward trend in the risk of British pre-marital births of about 10 per cent per annum.[71] It is studies of non-marital fertility which include both labour market variables (employment and/or income and welfare benefits) which find the strongest significant relationships between unwed motherhood and welfare levels, particularly when it is male earning opportunities and thus women's potential income from marriage which are juxtaposed to welfare. Thus, Mikhail S. Bernstam and Peter L. Swan found that, in America between 1960 and 1980, illegitimacy was low where both market wages and the probability of earning these wages was high relative to the level of welfare benefits, and vice versa.[72]

At the very least, if young workers are unable to find work or wages that might support a family, and the public assistance system is there to fill the gap with a basic income, women faced with the precariousness of men's support, but with means to support themselves, even minimally, may opt for parenting outside marriage, divorce or casual relationships. In turn, this further reduces the probability of marriage. Of course the effect is likely to be larger for women whose own personal economic, as well as marital, options are limited, especially in view of the fact that, while male employment and earnings facilitate marriage and marital births, female employment and earnings act as a barrier. The higher a woman's pay, the higher her opportunity costs, and so the higher the wages forgone from the employment interruption if she gets pregnant and has the child, instead of an abortion. With good economic prospects, teenagers have something to lose by having a baby, and are motivated to defer having children, in the same way that the pursuit of living standards has acted, for centuries, as the great family planner of the Western world.[73] American women from the Panel Study of Income Dynamics with higher predicted incomes (from themselves or their husbands) at 25, were less likely to have had children out-of-wedlock as teenagers.[74] While, here as elsewhere, women in states with higher public assistance were more likely to have had such births, a dollar of their own family income weighed more than one from AFDC.

But those whose earning capacity is low may not be able to better themselves much, if at all, through employment. Even the available employment may provide as little in the way of satisfaction as it does in terms of living standards. Out-of-wedlock births are everywhere, and overwhelmingly, concentrated among least educated women or those least likely to be able to support themselves and their babies. The British Women and Employment Study showed how women in jobs were about four times more likely to give birth before marriage than those continuing their education, but only half as likely as women who were in neither further education nor employment.[75]

In the circumstances, exercising the reproductive function, is something interesting to do, and for which a secure income of sorts is provided. Lower class women have often started childbearing early in life anyway: marrying the 'first man who comes along'. She is doing what most women want to do at some time or another, having children and looking after them herself, things which she might not be able to do at all if she waited to get married. In the middle class the disgrace of illegitimacy has been tied to personal and family aspirations, while the working class girl loses only some of her limited options by having an illegitimate child: she is not going to make a better marriage or improve her status either way.[76] Most unwed mothers conceive and deliver their babies deliberately, not accidentally. They do not necessarily have children to qualify for benefits, but they are well aware of the role which these play in supporting them.

Babies are almost always warmly welcomed by the family (who may have no other prospect of grandchildren) and many grandmothers will take care of the baby. As Elijah Anderson reports, these girls:

> have their independence, a welfare check, and food stamps (they may gain love and attention from young men by giving them a portion of the check).[77]

They can dress up their babies and show them off: "in their own eyes proving that they are managing just fine, living out their version of a decent life style". But, the 'prize baby' is not "usually the prize of first choice for many of these girls". This is more likely to be "upward mobility, the good life, having a family on the middle-class model ... to go to college or land a job down town". If they make do with what they have at their disposal, they really:

> ... want to be married to a good man ('someone who will treat me right') and settle down in a nice neighbourhood ... when a girl does become engaged to be married, relatives and friends express excitement and approval of her prospective life, particularly of the wedding ceremony itself. But this seldom happens. The dream of the good life usually unravels when the young men cannot come through as viable providers and husbands. Thus many girls settle for babies and part-time fathers.

For the man, presumptive fatherhood is not only a proof of sexual prowess which gives him 'street cred', but his loose connection to the woman allows him to maintain the free life style so valued by the peer group.

> He may reason that he is much better off remaining single, 'staying home with mama', and maintaining his freedom 'to come as I want and to go as I please'. Given his limited employment prospects such a resolution may afford him a better alternative than 'playing house' and being 'tied down with kids, bills, and all that'. Thus he has a distinct incentive for playing his role of father and 'husband' part-time.[78]

An Explosive Combination?

Where chronic destabilisation of male earnings is accompanied by an expansion of programmes supporting broken families there is likely to be a large shift from one location, or welfare system, to another. As, in the UK, adverse labour market conditions and the retreat from a tax system based on ability to pay have been allied to a complex system of means-tested reliefs and selective benefits skewed heavily towards lone parents, this adds to the disintegrative pressures under which more and more actual or prospective parents operate as they move into the orbit of income -related benefits.

While pre-school children generally tend to deter divorce, in poor families the presence of a young child and all the additional economic demands is correlated with break up. One in three couples reported a marked deterioration in their relationship when the man became unemployed, with one or other party contemplating leaving or having done so at some time, compared to only 3 per cent for controls.[79] People in low-income families experience considerably more tension and stress, and associations between divorce and family debts are high.

With the husband's contribution already low, or negative (in terms of the subsidies women can command as lone parents), there is little or no deprivation for a woman seeking dissolution and a:

> ... selfish beneficiary would be willing to increase her own income at the expense of family income if the increase exceeds the contribution from her benefactor".[80]

She will often be financially better off leaving the marriage precisely in those straitened circumstances where small matters of economics are likely to loom large in a couple's lives. Unlike the man who will lose home and children, and therefore is heavily deterred from divorce, the woman will keep both. Means-tested payments to mothers are reduced when earnings increase, but are raised, and other help is added at every income level, when fathers do not support children. Thus, as Gary Becker describes, the financial wellbeing of recipients is increased by children, but decreased by marriage.

In Britain a man has to provide as much as the lone mother's total from Income Support and other benefits, or her Family Credit income when in work, plus his own keep, if a woman is not going to take on a liability in marrying him. Progressively fewer and fewer young men will have net earnings high enough to clear the 'marriage trap', as marriage is transformed from an institution designed to protect children into one which particularly penalises low-income parents whose children would benefit from it most.

In 1992 a full-time manual worker aged between 21 and 24 had median earnings of £212 gross—meaning that a half of his age group would have earned less. If he were married with two small children his total net income would be £187.90. He was not entitled to any Family Credit, rent rebate or community charge benefit so that the couple had £147.38 after their rent and local taxes were paid, or less if we assume more than the lowest rent, and they would have had none of the health and education exemptions available to those on means-tested benefits. In comparison, a lone parent earning just £80 from a part-time job had a total net income of £159.81 (she got £54.81 Family Credit, an extra £5.80 one-parent benefit and £5.12 rent rebate). After paying her rent and community charge she had £124.56. Should the young husband earn below the median for his age group, or £188 a week, the maximum that qualifies for any Family Credit, his family would have had £131.54 after rent and community charge, while a lone mother had almost the same amount, or £131.25 after earning £130 a week. (On £188 she would have £142.66.)[81] From 1994, with up to £40 in income disregarded for childcare costs, she could get £163.31 for a part-time job paying £75 (see p. 18).

Looming in the background is a labour market in which the full-time male job, once meant to support a family, is being replaced by part-time female jobs. What was once a supplement to the main wage, providing additional, not base, family income, is being converted into the only declared support of a household. Employers have incentives to switch to part-time work as, if they pitch the wage and hours right, they have substantial wage subsidies from Family Credit. In Bill Jordon and colleagues' study of low-income families,[82] these inhabited a world where men's employment was unstable and risky and the demand for male labour unpredictable, in contrast to the buoyant demand for female workers. Only 12 of the men had regular full-time jobs, and they were preoccupied by the insecurity of their position: living in fear of redundancy, of being put onto short-term contracts and cast onto the casual and fragmented labour market.

Men faced with this situation have not been entirely without strategies to justify their family membership, many of them involving the disappearance of more economic transactions into the black economy. For unemployed and low-paid men, undeclared cash work becomes a legitimate way of getting out of the traps which frustrate the active worker who wants to be a successful breadwinner and stay with his family without making them worse off as a result. If the labour market did not sustain their requirements for a decent full-time job with adequate wages, and the benefits system meant their family had to go without, men in the Bill Jordan study fulfilled their obligation to provide a 'proper' income for the family from money derived from anything from breeding animals to decorating to hunting rabbits. Others, more ambitious as well as more ruthless, find that professional crime provides the comfortable living standard and entry into business once supplied through more conventional channels of social mobility.

Marriage Without Children

In accounting for lone parenthood, we add the big fall in marital fertility to the drop in the marriage rate and a certain increase in the propensity of single women to have babies. While it may have become easier to have children outside marriage, economic imperatives have made children increasingly incompatible with marriage. The result is dual fertility markets, as marital and non-marital fertility diverge.

Middle-class and, indeed, respectable working-class people have long believed that adults should refrain from having children unless they can care for them properly. This has meant not having children unless the mother was married and the father could support them. If income was insufficient, then people should restrict their fertility, since a certain living standard is the basis for 'responsible parenthood'. On the face of it, it all seems to impose impossible conditions, considering the direct and opportunity costs of children. However, a multitude of adjustments in the structure of employment, taxation and services, were built up and varied over time, and endeavoured to ensure that on the whole, most of those who acted reasonably prudently would have resources in terms of time and income to rear a smallish family without privation or undue strain.

However, with the dissolution of such measures as supported the family up to the 1970s, the result is that, while those who obey the traditional behavioural norms about family building may be far less likely to have out-of-wedlock births or become dependent on public assistance, they are also far more likely to have no children at all, or only one. At the same time, the structure of poverty subsidies now ensure that reproduction continues and expands outside marriage. The choice is not simply between a living standard without children or relative poverty with them, but also marriage without children or lone parenthood with them.

The rise in women's net earnings in relation to men's has been a major contributor to the way in which births have been insufficient to replace the population since the mid-1970s.[83] As women stayed in the labour market after marriage, equal pay and the elimination of gender differentiation further increased their labour force participation, but made childrearing into a most expensive use of the mother's time in terms of the returns forgone from virtually any paid occupation. The relative cost of children is significantly affected by changes in the value of married women's time, because this cost is a major part of the total cost of producing and rearing children. This means that the number of children is strongly negatively related to the wage rate of wives, while it is positively related to the earnings of husbands.

When he has a higher earning capacity, the husband gives his time to paid employment, and this makes housework 'cheaper' when supplied by the wife. In turn, increases in the husband's earnings raise the value of the wife's time at home. But with higher women's wages, the incentive for wives to work outweighs the disincentive for them not to, even when their husbands may be as highly paid. The couple can afford fewer children, because the woman's increased earnings potential also increases the cost in terms of earnings forgone. The higher a woman's earnings at marriage, the older she is at the time of her first birth and the smaller her family—if any.

Initially, the postponement of children after marriage, with the woman making profitable use of her marketable skills before withdrawing from work, seemed to promise couples the chance of starting a family off on a higher living standard than they might have on the basis of the man's wages alone. However, a dedicated two-income strategy has become increasingly necessary to cover household basics or maintain living standards. This makes the double income household probably the most effective contraceptive ever devised. Prices, particularly of housing, have risen to absorb two salaries and, as the jobs market has changed, wages have adjusted to equality through lower, unisex rates. By 1982, 80 per cent of childless couples under 30 had two earners, with the prospect of the loss of a goodly proportion of their income just at the point where there would be more people to support.

Of course, many husbands have still found it possible to make good some of the loss with extra effort. The 1991 survey of people in their mid-30s for the National Child Development Study showed that married men's median hourly earnings were higher (£7.20) than those of single men (£6.60), single women (£6.30) or married childless women full-time workers (£6.60). This is something which is heavily disapproved of and which labour force monitoring by 'equality action' programmes is out to prevent.[84] Moreover, again, taxation has exacerbated, rather than mitigated, the adverse effects of workplace equality on the capacity of couples to found families. Most obvious are exemptions for single people in local taxation. But the income tax threshold for one earner has been lower than for the combined income of a couple when both are employed. The higher tax bill meant that one-earner families with young children needed a wage of £21,283 in 1993 for a modest family budget in northern England, compared to £19,529 for two-earner families.[85]

The proposal of the 1986 Treasury Green Paper to allow transferability of the basic personal tax allowance between spouses would have involved some compensation for families with one main earner, just as it would have eased the poverty and unemployment traps faced by lower-income couples.[86] Moving in the opposite direction, the discrepancy between the taxes paid by one and two earner families has grown in the 1990s with freezing and now the removal of the marriage allowance. This pushes the ratio of tax allowances for one- and two-earner couples from 1½ to 2½, towards a more asymmetrical ratio of 1 to 2. This will increase couples' reliance on double incomes, and the difficulties of having a child within marriage will be racheted up. Moreover, with fathers taxed on the same basis as single, childless people, the income left to working families will bring more into the means-tested benefit system. Its unemployment, poverty and marriage traps will be enhanced by the same tax move as, at the same time, the position of the lone parent is greatly improved by additional allowances.

4

By Chance or Design?

Summary: *The breakdown of the traditional family is sometimes described as an irreversible trend, as if it is not related to public policy and economic factors. This is to treat reproductive behaviour as if it were different from all other life choices. The increasing adoption of non-traditional family types may not represent people's first choices so much as the most viable options open to them. While most people still regard traditional family life as the ideal, tolerance for other lifestyles has increased as the legal, religious and cultural barriers to divorce and extra-marital childbearing have been removed. Those who have experienced family breakdown are more tolerant of it in others, and more likely to repeat the cycle. In an attempt to justify or make the best of their own experience, they are more likely to denigrate the traditional family. Changes in divorce law have rendered the marriage contract virtually meaningless. Claims that it is not the role of the state to regulate relationships ignore the fact that mating and reproduction have been subject to regulation in every known society. The marriage allowance—the last recognition of marriage left in taxation—is regarded as a 'pot of gold' from which other areas of public expenditure could be funded. The Child Support Agency has won feminist approval because it opens up the prospect of an additional guaranteed income for mothers without having to have the father around.*

Embracing the Inevitable?

S O FAR, the evidence suggests that family disruption and decline owe much to policy-induced changes in incentives. The welfare state interacts with men's unemployment and earnings to disfavour marriage, and a cycle of financial stress on families has been enormously furthered by increasingly discriminatory taxation as well as by the abandonment of protection in labour and housing markets. There is a direct link between the withdrawal of government support for families, smaller family size, the dramatic rise in single adults, and the increasing incidence of family breakdown.[1]

Suggestions that family trends owe a great deal to the actions of policymakers—whether or not the outcomes were intended—are contrary to the dogma that government is incapable of influencing developments in this field. It may seem particularly unusual to pay special attention to the economic basis of family life. Despite the way in which people are forever discussing what they can afford, even many of those who give pride of place to the role of economics in behaviour are among the first to deny that material considerations make any difference to family and marital decisions.[2] The belief that family trends cannot be explained in economic terms shades into the belief that these are beyond understanding, yet there is no reason why they are any more unintelligible or beyond human influence than other social or physical phenomena.

To emphasise the extent to which economic factors influence people's decisions about marriage and childbearing is not to say that money is the only consideration, or the most important consideration. A host of factors are involved in the process of family formation and family stability and these affect each other. However, a pool of securely employed males is usually a necessary condition for a viable marriage market, just as the capacity to run a household which does not absorb two wages facilitates marital childbearing.[3]

In spite of this we are repeatedly told that people just do what they want to do; that "Today's plurality is the consequence of personal lifestyle decisions",[4] or, according to Malcolm Wicks, when he was director of the Family Policies Studies Centre, that:

> There are fewer marriages, more cohabitation, more children born out-of-wedlock, high divorce rates and more one-parent families. These are powerful forces and, faced with them, the governments are relatively powerless. The trends of the last 12 years were not for turning.[5]

At this point, an *is*, or a *will be*, tends to slip into an *ought*, and we often find standards being read off from the direction of trends, which we are bidden to embrace and accommodate just because they are happening. Extrapolations which have 50 per cent of children being reared outside the conventional family after the turn of the century are presented as if projections were prophecies, and these were already established facts which, furthermore, possessed a kind of moral authority which we are obliged to work towards. Hence, it is not just impossible to 'squeeze the toothpaste back into the tube'; we are meant to help history squeeze it out.

Change or Decay?

But nobody has to accept the morality of the future simply because it is the morality, *or behaviour*, of the future, even were this unalterable. It should be obvious that the family, as a moral norm, is something to be striven for and supported independently of how many people's lives actually approximate to it at any one time. At least those who argue that the growth of 'father-free' families is progress in the fight against gender distinctions and women's oppression are not insisting that their preferences are foisted onto them by events. They represent family trends as a break for freedom made by brave women who have "refused to marry to legitimate their sexual lives" or "were able to take control of their own fertility, by choosing to have children outside of marriage". Under this scenario, "women's refusal to marry is not simply a personal choice or question of 'lifestyle', it is a crucial *political* choice" and part of establishing an "oppositional culture".[6]

There is much talk about a diversity of family forms or ways in which families are simply changing and not breaking down. Those who may not see it quite like this are portrayed as projecting an ideal onto the real world, where only an unrepresentative minority now choose to live in the conjugal, or nuclear, family. But, without a practical definition or reference point, it is made difficult for anyone—whether for or against the family—even to *describe* what is supposed to be changing, or *explain* what is happening. A particular conception of the family might be a moral norm, but it can also be a workable definition for purposes of investigation. It is possible to talk of the family system of the Mumbobumbo tribe, and whether it is breaking up, without approving of how they organise their reproductive life.

Moreover, it also allows us to make distinctions between what people want and what they get, where their situations may represent an inability to achieve a desired goal, rather than the invention of another model or a challenge to traditional features of family life.[7]

Left wing or 'progressive' commentators like to represent government as struggling to uphold the family against a tide of popular rejection. This does not fit the facts. In times of good labour market opportunities, especially for men, favourable tax *régime* and affordable housing, we find family formation and family stability invariably increasing, with rising rates of marriage and marital births. In contrast, the displacement of births outside marriage is very sporadic in time and place, and shows little continuity, even in the same nation.[8]

This distribution suggests that there is little stable preference for non-marital childbearing, given the availability of other options. Whether it occurs anywhere, at any time, to any great degree, depends upon the existence of special subsidies or incomes for lone mothers or—as in the early industrial revolution—demand for child labour from extended kin.

If people are really repudiating the Western marriage system as a matter of choice, then we must assume that they have a very low preference for marriage, marital childbearing and prosperity for themselves and their offspring. "Their preference must be the opposite to those of the rest of humankind over millennia. ... Escaping many long-term opportunities ... they must be disutility maximizers".[9]

As William Julius Wilson complains for America, the focus on female (or black) assertion and the definition of the problem in sexual or racial terms has effectively diverted attention away from economic shifts and their impact, particularly on poor communities. This makes it difficult to appreciate the extent to which economic forces and public policy decisions are bearing down on the family.[10] It is perfectly possible that if it were economically more feasible for people to marry and have children, marriage and the marital birthrate would rise—rather than it being "unlikely that any political party will be capable of persuading this young generation of parents to return to the nuclear family".[11]

Dominant opinion has, anyway, been running ahead of the statistics in an eagerness to announce the demise of the family. Even if all other circumstances in which children are reared are deemed separate 'family forms', assertions that marriage or two parents are not statistically 'normal' have been factually incorrect. As writers for the Family Policy Studies Centre were relegating the British family to the past as something that "used to evoke a picture of a husband and wife and their children living together in one household",[12] it was publishing figures (for

1987) showing 22 per cent of the population living as married couples with no children, 44 per cent as married couples with dependent children and 12 per cent as married couples with independent children—or 78 per cent of the population in all. The Economic and Social Research Council and National Children's Bureau presented the *Life at 33* survey of 1991 with the claim that "The oft stated preference of government for the nuclear family simply does not represent reality for a large proportion of the young families" since 24 per cent of women had been a lone parent at some point.[13] The 63 per cent of respondents in their first marriage were ignored.

Many of the diverse family forms which we hear so much about merely represent stages in the life cycle. Even if everybody got married, stayed married and had the number of children they wanted, we would still have only around a third of households containing dependent children. Increasing longevity means that people live for decades after their children have grown up and left home, in a world which also contains all the couples who have yet to have children and the single people yet to marry.[14]

Nevertheless, whilst the nuclear family remains the statistical norm, it is also true that the number of nuclear family households is decreasing, and that not all of this decrease can be accounted for by the changing age structure of the population. So what are the new, emerging family forms which we are hearing about? Malcolm Wicks and Kathleen Kiernan describe these new families in terms of "cohabitation, of having children outside of marriage, of marital breakdown, and the rise in the number of lone mothers".[15] However, there is nothing new about these groupings—they have always existed. Whatever sort of family structure is regarded as the norm in a society, there have always been irregular marriages, concubinage, adulteries and prohibited couplings. The really original aspect of statistics showing changing household types in recent years is the growth in *one-person* households from 14 per cent of all households in 1961 to 27 per cent in 1992, with the biggest increase for men under pensionable age. However, this is not a new family type, but *the absence of any family at all*.

The one-parent family is the result of the break-up of families, or procreation outside of family structures, not a new family form. Despite attempts to find cultural precedents for the institutionalisation of the lone mother as the norm, we have no reason to revise Malinowski's view of the fatherless family as an aberration (see p. vi). Patricia Hewitt and Penelope Leach insist that "in the Afro-Caribbean community ... female headed families are commonplace and are not regarded as second best",[16] and Janet Finch tells us that the "Mother-headed household is a cultural norm for people of Caribbean or African origin ... a sign of a strong family life rather than an undesirable modification". However, the attitudes of Geoff Dench's West Indian respondents to arrangements other than the nuclear family "were generally less than enthusiastic".[17]

The accelerating decay of the traditional family unit and the relative paucity of children must be seen in relation to the worsening economic conditions of childhood and the increasing stresses on those of childbearing age. These are all pointers to developments that are eroding or undermining the capacity of the society to replace itself adequately and ensure the quantity and quality of its population. One writer gives the game away when, after intoning the orthodoxy that "the traditional nuclear family is but one form together with many other forms", then describes how children often now "cannot firmly rely on a continuity of care and protection provided by their parents ... Family relationships ... have been individualised. Modern family life is unstable".[18]

Breaking the Barriers

Whatever the attitudes of influential élites, the population at large has been disinclined to accept that divorce, homosexuality, staying single or childless are desirable goals. However, while most people have doggedly continued to value and desire marriage, parenthood and stable family life, nevertheless we have seen a shift towards tolerating or permitting previously pro-scribed behaviour.[19]

It is widely believed that cohabitation is beneficial as a preparation for marriage. Over 70 per cent of people believe that a child needs both parents to grow up properly, but young mothers are as likely as not to accept that a woman may have a baby outside of any stable relationship.[20] While 88 per cent of Britain's teenagers in the early 1990s expected to get married, a quarter of girls also thought they had a good chance of becoming single parents.[21] If girls accept the possibility that they can become single parents, it is something which raises the probability of becoming one significantly—or three-fold, according to American research.[22]

As Norman Dennis and George Erdos correctly observe, youths have lost the:

> taken for granted project for life of responsibility for their own wife and children. Their expectations had ceased to be automatically geared to unavoidable parenthood.[23]

Mark Testa's work on inner city Chicago is instructive: while he shows that men with stable work are now twice as likely to marry as those without, the disparity in marriage rates between employed and jobless men was smaller in the past because:

> In earlier years, the social stigma of illegitimacy counter-balanced economic considerations in the decision to marry. As the norms of legitimacy weakened, marriage rates dropped precipitously among chronically jobless men as couples no longer felt obliged to legitimate the birth of a child for social reasons.[24]

Women's growing ability to control their own fertility, and the emphasis on their exclusive rights to decide if, and when, they have children and if they should carry a pregnancy to term, may also have weakened men's feelings that they are morally obliged to marry their pregnant girlfriend. If a woman can get the pill or an abortion, but chooses not to, her "boyfriend is unlikely to feel that her pregnancy is his responsibility"[25]—particularly when he is not in the best position to provide for a family.[26]

The fact that what used to be regarded as the prerogatives of the married state, like regular sexual companionship, are now routinely available to unmarried people makes the absence of marriage easier to bear. As economic conditions make it more difficult to have and rear children within marriage, more people will settle for the next best thing or least worst option, even if only a small minority would have actively pursued it. There is continual assurance that lust is enough for sex and the expectation of readily available copulation is remorselessly cultivated. This gives men the *prospect,* if not always the realisation, of easy gratification, without the onerous burden of family responsibilities. Women who would otherwise have been likely to remain childless spinsters, if potential husbands were scarce, now smoothly progress from *can do*, to *may do,* to *will* have a baby alone. Women's magazines have righteously espoused the cause of lone parents and presented them as heroic role models. "So what do you think you need a man for?" asks a giveaway magazine, as it trumpets the virtues of singlehood: "Babies? Think artificial insemination".[27]

The fact that as recently as the 1970s J. Busfield and M. Paddon reported on the way in which marriage, children, parenthood and families were inextricably linked, particularly in working-class communities,[28] shows how these beliefs—that marriage confers various rights and statuses including the right to have children—have weakened within a short space of time.

It is no paradox that, in the past, families received considerable economic protection, while individuals were meant to desist from marriage and childbearing if their personal circumstances were not right for family foundation. As family life was a commitment which the state supported so, by the same token, the individual did not undertake this unless he or she was in a position properly to meet the responsibilities involved. In our times, the flattening of the tax structure marks the way in which family life has been publicly relegated to just another matter of taste or personal inclination, without a communal basis or worth. However, at the same time that children have become a consumer choice, which it would be 'unfair' to support before any others, everyone has also acquired a right to exercise this 'choice', along with any others. In this children simply become a means to adult fulfilment or gratification, and not the repositories or carriers of a valued way of life or the future of a people.

Not only the erosion of the significance attached to the married state, but the declining influence of religious, moral and legal obstacles, including stigma, to marital dissolution and illegitimacy, has left individuals freer to respond in the face of apparent advantages and disadvantages of various options. There is nothing new about stress within marriage, but whether or not marital stress leads to divorce depends on the barriers which are erected to deter certain courses of action as well as the alternatives available. The barriers have largely come down as divorce law has ceased to be a daunting process requiring the establishment of an objectively defined fault of marital behaviour. Instead, the onus has shifted onto individuals to decide if their marriage has ended, knowing that they have easy access to cheap and approved ways of splitting up.

In the run up to the major divorce law reform of 1969 divorce
was promoted as a sort of undertaker for the decent burial of
dead marriages. This rejected a causal link between the law and
divorce rates, on the grounds that this confused divorce with
marital breakdown. Instead, the latter was envisaged as some
kind of naturally determined and inevitable phenomenon.
According to this view the law could not have an influence on
marriage since, by definition, it merely gave formal legal
recognition to a situation that had already taken place. Divorce
on demand would therefore reflect the true state of marriage.
Impediments to divorce permitted the existence of 'hole in the
corner' unions and illegitimacy, so that informal unions and out-
of-wedlock births could be expected to decrease with easier
divorce.

But liberalisation meant that the law had altered the nature
of the contract it terminates. The new norms of behaviour it
incorporated made all marriages provisional, leading spouses to
anticipate independence, and be more ready to jump if times got
tough. By the same token, people are dissuaded from investing
in the marital relationship. John Ermisch, who gives a decisive
role to divorce law in the way in which lone parenthood went on
the rise in the 1970s, emphasises the way in which easier divorce raises the likelihood of dissolution, not least because people
effectively use marriage as a base to go on searching for a better
match or other opportunities.[29] In turn, marriage has less
influence over future behaviour as there are fewer reasons to get
married in the first place. A self-perpetuating legal process is set
in motion under which, as Ruth Deech describes it:

> Every increase in the divorce rate results in greater familiarity
> with divorce as a solution to marital problems, more willingness
> to use it and to make legislative provision for its aftermath. The
> pressure on the divorce system leads to a relaxation of practice
> and procedure in divorce, then to a call for a change in the law
> in order to bring it into line with reality, and then to yet
> another increase in divorce.[30]

Surveys have consistently shown public opinion lagging behind
the process of the progressive easing of the divorce laws. Certainly the population have never accepted the reformers' conclusion that marriage is superfluous and most people are unaware
that this has, in effect, been the drive behind new legislation
and administrative moves since 1969. However, attitudes have

moved in the permissive direction after each relaxation of controls. Moreover, attitudes towards marital dissolution or out-of-wedlock births shift as more people become involved in these trends.[31] At the same time, the media has set out to 'normalise' promiscuity, illegitimacy and homosexuality, with the biggest predicted effect being on those most dependent upon television.

Divorced and remarried people have more tolerant attitudes to separation and divorce, as do unmarried mothers for rearing children without fathers. Data from the 1987 British Election Survey and the 1989 British Attitudes Survey suggested marked differences in attitudes to marriage between employed families and an 'underclass' sample of long-term means-related benefit recipients. The latter were less inclined to suppose that people who want children should get married (47 per cent to 64 per cent), or that single parents are less able to bring up their children (33 per cent to 60 per cent).[32]

Illegitimacy and divorce lead to their own greater acceptance, in a series of feedback loops. As more young adults are raised in disrupted homes, this increases their probability of divorce or of becoming single mothers. As divorce and single motherhood become more commonplace, familiarity increases tolerance and the individual faces less opposition. As social and economic conditions foster family fragmentation, the feedback helps to ensure that divorce and unwed motherhood are seen as viable alternatives to marriage in the context of increasing numbers of divorces and single mothers. This contributes to a climate of expectations in which family trends appear to develop a momentum of their own: the more divorces and unwed births there are, the more there will be.

When people do not attain their objectives they may not only want to present what they have ended up with in the best possible light, but also to dismiss the original expectations as unnecessary or unworthy anyway. Up into the 1990s, the denigration and mockery of the family by middle-class élites failed to make inroads into a solid 90 per cent support for marriage as an institution among the general population. If this fell suddenly (with a rise from 9 per cent to 16 per cent agreeing that marriage was dead), then it is accounted for by rejection from nearly a quarter of those at the bottom of the social hierarchy, where it has become particularly difficult to establish and maintain families at all.[33]

While the disintegration and diminution of the family unit owes much to the way in which its economic base has been largely destroyed, this divestment has gone hand in hand with legal disestablishment. Labour market, macro-economic developments and tax and benefit policies, not only affect behaviour but, in so doing, also embody and promote certain assumptions and attitudes. In a pertinent illustration of how economic variables have a decisive impact on family patterns and parental behaviour, Elijah Anderson describes how the role model of the family man has been undermined with the collapse of the financial health of poor areas. The work opportunities for men in the inner cities and mining areas, once underpinned conventional working-class values. In their absence, street values, represented by fast sex, violence and crime, easily become predominant. The father of the working class family:

> ...was once the epitome of decency in inner-city neighbourhoods. Strongly supported by a vibrant manufacturing economy, he had relatively stable means. His acknowledged role in the community was to teach, support, encourage and, in effect, socialise young men to meet their responsibilities regarding work, family life, the law and common decency.[34]

But, as meaningful employment becomes scarce for young men, the 'old head' loses prestige and authority. Boys conclude that his lessons about conventional family life and the work ethic—incessantly assaulted as these are by a nihilistic media—are no longer relevant. The new, attractive role model is:

> The embodiment of the street, he is young, often the product of the street gang, and indifferent at best to the law and traditional values. If he works, he does so grudgingly. More likely he makes ends meet ... in the drug trade or some other area of the underground economy. He derides conventional family life; he has a string of women but feels little obligation towards them or the children he has fathered.[35]

The failure to protect families in the face of economic changes over the last couple of decades and the propensity to add to these by shifting the tax burden onto parents as part of a wholesale dispersal of entitlements built up over time, cannot be separated from the way in which the family has come under historically unprecedented attack.

Nothing We Can Do?

As the family weakens, this provides the *prima facie* evidence for some commentators that it cannot be supported, whereas in the past protective steps would have been taken. "The number of one-parent families has grown rapidly" says John Ermisch, "and it appears that there is little that policy can do to reduce their numbers"[36]—which hardly follows. Certainly, he is concerned that the lack of a father's income, and the possible intergenerational effects of spending part of childhood in a one-parent family, both point to a need for policies that reduce the number of one-parent families, but insists that this must not be done as "such policies may either be ineffective or infringe basic liberties in British society. Even if they can be effective, they will not eliminate one-parent families".[37] But it is surely no argument for inaction in the face of any social, physical or environmental problem, from disease to air pollution, litter or crime, that this will not eliminate it.

Moreover, the argument that "it is difficult to devise policy changes that significantly reduce the number of one-parent families without having other effects that are undesirable"[38] must be distinguished from factual claims that these policy changes will not succeed. But both objections are run together to suggest that the only options left to us are policies "directed at improving the living standards of one-parent families", and that basically "the primary social problem associated with one-parent families is their low income".[39]

Since there has been increasing discrepancy in support for one- and two-parent families, where couples have become progressively disadvantaged, it is difficult to see how it is undesirable to redress the balance by supporting child-rearing by two parents as well as by one. It is usually assumed that policies aimed at stemming the rise in lone parents can only take the form of draconian cuts to their benefits, perhaps because this is the course suggested by welfare critics like Charles Murray. His answer to welfare dependency and illegitimacy is "The Alexandrian solution: cut the knot, for there is no way to untie it", by scrapping the entire federal welfare and income support structure for working-age persons including AFDC, Medicaid, Food Stamps, subsidised housing, disability insurance, and the rest.[40] He would leave unemployment insurance in its original contributory form. Otherwise, apart from family and friends, there is just a hard-core local welfare system which can employ "fine-grained judgements based on personal knowledge". This could convert:

> ... a large proportion of the younger generation of hardcore unemployed into steady workers making a living wage ... drastically reduce births to single teenage girls ... reverse the trend-line in the breakup of families ... measurably increase the upward socio-economic mobility of poor families.[41]

However, the ability of family supporters to deliver a living wage depended upon an intricate structure of protective and compensatory measures, not least fiscal. With general concessions for the cost of dependants, it is possible to deal with poverty without creating disincentives. Otherwise, work, rising income or marriage may be pointless to the parent if this means losing their poor relief. It is then easy to conclude that—if not coercion—then the abolition of public assistance must be the only possible answer to the incentives problem.

Charles Murray is damning about the perverse incentives of public assistance, though not so strong on the role of universal recognition for family responsibilities in ensuring the viability of families, and overcoming incentives problems—or how the removal of such measures may be linked to both poverty and family dissolution. Moreover, conservatives tend to be too dismissive of the role of labour market developments in family instability, preferring to associate both this and declining employment to welfare alone. As David T. Ellwood remarks, any choice model suggests that both can play a role, and that if one economic factor is important, another is likely to be as well.[42]

Those who argue that selective welfare makes no difference to family breakdown or out-of-wedlock births have pointed to the way in which real AFDC levels fell in America after the mid-1970s, entitlement was cut back and the number of children on the programme actually declined—but this did not stem the continued rise in lone parenthood, or increasing child poverty. However, all recipients got Medicaid—unlike many poor working families—and housing assistance. Food stamps did not lose so much of their value and the programme was expanded again by the late 1980s after being cut at the beginning of the decade, and benefit levels were raised higher than at any time in the programme's history. As Mikhail S. Bernstam and Peter L. Swan point out, the sustained increase in white, non-marital fertility in the second half of the 1970s and early 1980s, despite the decline in real benefits, is partly attributable to both the fall in young male incomes in relation to welfare and a decline in expected permanent incomes due to rising unemployment figures.[43] But, for whatever reason, the overall rise in the proportion of female headed families did slacken through the 1980s; the divorce rate was down and the overall out-of-wedlock birthrate steadied—although both were on the rise again by the end of the decade.

Moreover, even if cuts in lone-parent benefits reduce out-of-wedlock births, it does not follow that stable two-parent families will increase to the same degree. It is feasible that marriage rates and births to married women will go on falling. Withdrawing all assistance for lone mothers, or cutting this to a very low level, might increase mortality and distress without much improvement in the formation rate and conditions of families. As Ellwood rightly observes, an important reason why American welfare cuts had little impact in the 1980s was because:

> It was not the behaviour of welfare recipients that was the source of the shifts. It was the behaviour of others, outside the welfare system. The hypothesis also points to the fact that a reduction in unmarried births should be but one goal of policy. Obviously, anything that can be done to reduce these births would help. But policies that could improve the position of married couples or make marriage look better may ultimately have a greater impact. For it is the behaviour of married couples that has changed the most.[44]

Casting Asunder

It might seem that "Common decency and elementary psychology ... call for more attention to the rewards offered for good behaviour"[45] where, if we helped two-parent families become more economically secure and cope more effectively, marriage would be more viable. And, as "the status of two-parent families improves, so the desirability of marrying, having children, and remaining together increases".[46] Furthermore, history demonstrates that we are perfectly capable of instituting policies that affirm and promote more effective and secure two-parent families. But, as David T. Ellwood and Lawrence H. Summers sadly report: "We know of no serious policy that encourages family formation."[47] This is something brought home by the piles of reports on remodelling the British benefit system to support lone parents while there have been hardly any proposals for supporting the two-parent family.[48]

Denials that tax and benefits, or housing allocation, could possibly affect family structure often amount to pleas that nothing be done whilst, at the same time, any effects that proposed measures might have on the proportions of lone parents also tend to be disregarded or dismissed on grounds that all 'family forms' are equally valid. Some, like Malcolm Wicks, fret that "Inaction on family policy will mean more children suffering the traumas associated with family change and the social consequences will become apparent for all to see", and beg that "Something *should* be done".[49] But, apart from the package for lone parents and somewhere to put the children of mothers "needing and wanting employment", this amounts to counselling to enable people to come to terms with "the social revolution of family change" and help children adjust to the upheavals involved.

This attitude has been embedded in public policy since the 1969 divorce law allowed unilateral 'no fault' divorce. The replacement of legal restrictions which used to be defended as essential safeguards for the integrity of marriage as a lifelong union by ties of choice, terminable without any intervention by the community, made it equally irrelevant to design social security provisions for lone parents so as to avoid undermining marriage. Rejecting any necessity to uphold marriage, the only task has been to secure the interests of dependent children. The establishment of the Finer Committee, also in 1969, was in recognition of the claims of advocates of reform that if "in law, marriage would come to be a tenancy-at-will", this necessarily involved extensive state provision. As O.R. McGregor insisted, "A divorced man with a low income cannot maintain two wives and possibly two sets of children" and there were already men in prison for failing to observe maintenance orders. Thus:

> If the community permits divorce it must be prepared to meet the inevitable consequences of divorce... Rational reform implies modifications in attitudes towards the consequences of divorce. A marriage creates dependencies so also its dissolution may create social casualties which confront responsible people with conflicting

obligations that cannot be discharged because there is insufficient money to go round. Such casualties must be accepted at least as the temporary responsibility of social policy.[50]

In line with McGregor's reasoning, the Divorce Law Reform Act of 1969 was accompanied by the award to lone parents of a proportion of the married man's tax allowance, known as the 'additional person's allowance', with the full amount following in 1975-76, and one parent benefit from 1977-78. One 'tidying up' measure of the Matrimonial and Family Proceedings Act 1984 was the removal of the old obligation on the courts to leave the parties to divorce in the same economic position as they might be had the marriage not broken up. The type of case where the new 'clean break' procedures might apply was advertised as the short, childless marriage where the woman's earnings were uninterrupted, or there was sufficient capital to provide adequately for all concerned.

As might be expected, figures for the following years suggested a momentous change towards the 'clean break' approach with a large increase in applications for maintenance dismissed and a similar reduction in orders for payments.[51] The parliamentary opposition disliked the 1984 Act because the government had not legislated for the state to make the kind of sweeping provision for lone parents which it was felt to imply. But, if many of its extra-parliamentary supporters correctly saw it as a gateway to a necessary extension of state support, then the means-tested benefits system was being progressively adapted to accommodate the rising numbers of lone parents.

By this time, the Law Commission had come to see no value in retaining legal marriage, and has gone for final abolition in substance if not in title. As expressed by Brenda Hoggett, Law Commissioner, the law only dealt in measures for the protection of children and spouses which were as much applicable to the unmarried so:

> Logically we have already reached a point at which, rather than discussing which remedies should now be extended to the unmarried, we should be considering whether the legal institution of marriage continues to serve any useful purpose.[52]

Denying that this now had any communal basis or worth, the 1988 Law Commission report insisted that there was no more need to support marriage than "any other living arrangement".

As the final step towards effective abolition, the 1993 government Green Paper *Looking to the Future: Mediation and the
Grounds for Divorce* proposed that either spouse may initiate
divorce proceedings without going through the formality of
quoting any reason, and only 12 months need elapse to the final
decree as a time in which the parties can sort out the practical
arrangements.[53]

Although mating and reproduction have been subject to
regulation in all known societies, the Foreword to the Green
Paper denied that law could ever "prescribe the expectations
with which individuals enter marriage and so it cannot enforce
them", despite the fact that the purpose of marriage has always
been made abundantly clear by state and Church in terms of
mutual and permanent commitments between couples. Indeed,
rather than being an exception, marriage has exemplified the
way that, in lacking instinctual guides to action, human beings
create institutions to give coherence and continuity to their lives.
But while the defining framework of marriage transcends
transient feelings or inclinations, the law now seeks to define
marriage as existing in nothing but passing attraction. And, if
the individuals involved rapidly find that "reality may fall short
of the ideal", leading to "widespread disappointment and
disillusionment and, ultimately, breakdown", the law can no more
say when marriage is over than what it is. Its only task is to
provide mechanisms which adjust the parties' "living arrangements and their financial positions when things go wrong",[54] or
provide for the women and children.

Many people who still marry clearly do so under serious
misapprehensions. The declarations made are no longer required
in law, are not reflected in it and are regarded as purely
ceremonial. This has made marriage no more relevant than
cohabitation or boy and girlfriend relations, which is the logical
outcome of a moral neutrality which refuses to promote one type
of family structure over another. Under such a *régime*, the only
recognised 'family form' necessarily becomes a woman and her
children. Any arrangement she happens to have with a man or
men is irrelevant. In feminist terms, the family has been
'deconstructed' or dissolved into its constituent parts and
relationships. Otherwise, if respect was owed to any moral
principle or social structure and a woman had obligations
towards a husband or children, these would constitute such

'defects of the marital package' as have traditionally obstructed the expression of her needs.[55] At the same time, the removal of obligations makes marriage anomalous and irrelevant.

The Children Act

Continuing the process of deconstructing marriage, the Children Act 1989 gives the unmarried father a status almost equivalent to the married father and treats the two as identical in function. He can make an agreement with his 'partner' to recognise his 'parental responsibility' and give him a share in a child, without him living with the mother or being directly involved and taking part in the child's upbringing. In turn, a family "includes any person who has parental responsibility for the child and any person with whom he has been living". Any child, with leave of the court if he has "sufficient understanding", or appears to know what he wants, may revoke parental responsibility.[56]

Under the Act, lesbians have been granted parental rights, or "joint residence orders", through nomination by the children's mother. As described by the Children's Legal Centre, by "taking into account a child's actual relationships, as opposed to some abstract or ideological notion of what they should be,[57] it has deftly severed the age-old rooting of parenthood in marriage.

This is all presented as an enlightened policy where, instead of prescribing anything about what adults' sex lives, living arrangements or obligations towards each other should be, we simply 'regulate' parenting. On the face of it, the responsibility for determining parenthood is passed to the child, or is meant to emerge spontaneously from the situation in which he finds himself. It all suggests that social conventions and institutions are somehow contrary to the child's natural inclinations or interests, when in fact no society has ever left the survival, socialisation and affiliation of the young to the vagaries of *ad hoc* attachments.

Certainly, the disestablishment of marriage is inseparable from the weakening of the position of the married father. The children, essentially, are the natural property of the mother and, should she decide, for any reason or none, to abandon a marriage or dispense with a man, he must automatically leave the home and children. Hence, the authentication of all 'family forms' as equally valid means that, although single-parent families need not be perceived as preferred structures, they reflect the "reality of today's families".[58] It seems to follow that this current diversity of family forms, or mothers in any or no permutation of relations with adjunct men (or women) "means that the functions which the *traditional* or *model* family were supposed to perform will have to be recognised in new ways".[59] These become functions of the mother, and 'gender specific' wage labour and child welfare provisions must be designed in relation to the mother/child unit "because it is women who are in charge of reproduction".[60]

Simple logic also seems to point to fathers as just a nuisance or unnecessary complication, particularly to welfare service agencies. If family splits give us lone parents it may be better that, first as last, we simply deal with mothers. Thus, the National Children's Home reports how, under the pressure of debts, families break up, leaving women as lone parents with low incomes. It then observes how, "Even when families are not in debt, links have been found between who controls family finances and the level of family discord, with male control of money frequently tending to increase the level of family unhappiness" (although women actually had full control of finances in 78 per cent of its sample families). From this the conclusion is that: "policies aimed at helping *families* may best be targeted at supporting mothers", with increased benefits, "access to the labour market" and "childcare services which recognise child-rearing as a collective concern".[61]

Of course, at the same time as it is being planned out of existence in these ways, the reality is that the family remains the primary social unit, with a foremost responsibility for rearing its children. If husband and wife cover the tasks involved between them, then it should be possible to use tax policy and other measures to ensure that as many as possible can carry this out, if need be, on a minimum basis of one full-time worker without entering the public assistance system. But suggestions like transferable tax allowances, which could lower the tax burden when one parent withdraws from the labour force, tend to lead to accusations of unfairness to lone parents, in that such measures take advantage of marital interdependence. Either the proposal is abandoned, or it is suggested that the lone parent might receive the equivalent in cash, without the efforts of the second party. Again, this underscores how families and the mother/child unit are in competition. However, pleas for lone parents to receive a substantial range and degree of assistance, because they lack a second person, are usually combined with an emphatic insistence that two-parent families must receive no help at all to enable them to share parental responsibilities. As such, the mutual support which gives the two-parent family much of its point, particularly when it can be exercised in effective co-operation, is itself challenged.

Money and Power

The public may not be aware of how European Community directives on the equality of men and women in employment, pay, training and advancement, effectively negate marriage and the rearing of children at home. Consequently, while it is generally understood to be a normal, proper and an essential part of marriage that people share and share alike, and an obligation to maintain has been embedded in custom, law and ceremony, 'income dependency within couples' is now defined as a social problem crying out for detailed investigation and remedy. The Equal Opportunities Commission and European Commission have produced elaborate plans to eliminate the asymmetrical or complementary family and to:

> break into this vicious cycle and change the present relationship between child-care, gender and inequality of employment.[62]

The data provided by the National Child Development Study (whose subjects are now grown up) have been used to establish how many women are dependent on their partners and to what degree. The intention is not only to get some idea of the dimensions of this scourge but, most importantly, of "whether a woman has enough income to leave the relationship".[63] Further stages of investigation are under way to find out which "states of dependency are likely to be transitory or entrenched"[64] and to identify pathways out of dependence. Not that economic dependence is the only recognised way in which women are restricted, it being observed how:

> ... even if a woman does reach a specified level of income, however this is defined, she may still not feel able to leave the relationship for a range of reasons, including emotional dependency, consideration of the children, a lack of knowledge of other options and social pressure.[65]

It is also acknowledged in passing that human societies are webs of interdependencies—but these must go, for all that. Here the hostility to any division of domestic responsibilities at any time, and any mutual support, amounts to more than simply the repudiation of the basis of family life as a system of obligations, or a role for anything apart from occupational achievement in determining the individual's position and activities. The aim is to eradicate the most fundamental unit of civil society. Instead of the family providing meaning, attachment and, often, protection from the forces of the market and the state, women and children are always and only to derive their livelihood and condition directly from these impersonal sources. Income from a 'partner' is said to be more 'unreliable' than from the state or the market; it leads to 'feelings of insecurity and lack of control' and, of course, 'dependence' in families is defined as both impoverishing and oppressive.[66] Far from the family being important for political freedom, it is the source of subordination.

When family relations are analysed as aspects of the distribution of 'power' then, insofar as there is any exchanges of income and services or allocation of tasks, 'power' is seen to be distributed unequally. In turn, 'unequal power relations', or 'powerlessness' at home, feeds into 'powerlessness' in the marketplace. What is vehemently condemned is the 'widespread view that the *good* mother should not be employed until her children reach a certain age, and then possibly only on a part-time basis', and the notion that the "main role of the *good* father is to support his family financially through employment".[67] Given that mothers have taken part-time and temporary employment to make ends meet, this is seen as:

> not sufficient to achieve genuine economic independence in terms of the balance of economic power and equity of financial arrangements within families.[68]

Indeed, the common belief that male responsibility entails financial support for families is put "at the heart of the present crisis in family life" by Patricia Hewitt, Anna Coote and Harriet Harman,[69] while Joanna Foster, chairperson of the UK Council for the International Year of the Family, complains that the fact that "We're still carrying around the idea that the father is the breadwinner and the mother has to make the home ... is putting an intolerable strain on relationships".[70]

These people never ask themselves why other people's lives must conform to their preferences. Parents and children do best with arrangements of their choice which they feel comfortable with. It could as much or more be said that the present 'crisis' of family life is the result of people having to cope in circumstances they wished were different. In this, it is the increasing labour market marginality of males, not females, which has such profoundly negative implications for children.

The problem with the indictment of the male provider is that he is hardly using his wage power to make women dependent and subordinate, when childless married women and single men and women have much the same earnings. Children are the real problem. In being born to women and necessitating attentive care, it is they who are the ones holding back their mothers, married or not, from blazing their career paths. Has not the work of Clare Ward, Heather Joshi and Angela Dale on the National Child Development Study findings shown, to feminist satisfaction, how the majority of childless full-time working women (96 per cent) could be 'self-sufficient' in that they could easily 'get by' without the man on their present income. In comparison, only 55 per cent of the part-timers could be 'self-sufficient', and 93 per cent of the married mothers fully out of the workforce could not. Clearly, if "equal participation in the labour force is jeopardised by the domestic and child-related tasks that women tend to undertake",[71] putting mothers on a par with childless women means getting the children, not just husbands, out of the way.

Providing for Mothers

To alleviate the difficulties faced by lone parents, the question has turned upon whether policies should specifically target them, or mothers in general as an equal rights issue. Thus, the argument proceeds, were financial dependence within marriage to disappear, the problems faced by lone mothers would be solved, or greatly reduced, and children would not experience material deprivation. It seems that a wholesale liberation would be engineered if all women "could earn an income sufficient to support themselves and their children independently".[72] Then, if these self-sufficient mothers saw men as no more than casual associates—with a girl taught how "any man who might attach himself for part or all of the journey is not her destiny"—they would no longer be "victims of the ideal of marriage". There is also the suggestion that lone parenthood would be less of an economic burden for the state if, instead of supporting the "ever growing armies of girls on social security", it made the "best investment a government can make" and tried to "create a cultural expectation that all women will work all their lives—backed by childcare".[73]

Thus either the state takes over the childrearing to free mother for employment, or it provides a social benefit for all, irrespective of their connection with any particular man, as one way of giving women an independent income, sufficient to keep them out of poverty.[74] This assumes that every adult is completely financially independent and nobody shares their income, with no change in their benefit entitlements as they moved in and out of 'partnerships'.

One way might be to have an independent means-tested system. An alternative is a full basic guaranteed income which could meet every person's needs without a means test. This would replace all tax allowances and other benefits, and would require a tax on all other income of at least 70 per cent.[75]

However, both the fully fledged means-tested and basic income schemes have come to be seen from equal opportunities perspectives in terms of a dangerous "encouragement to women to stay at home".[76] They raise:

> ... in acute form a more general dilemma: the achievement of an independent income for women through the benefit system could undermine women's access to an independent income through paid employment.[77]

Suggestions for a parental care allowance for those rearing children at home, or even a parent benefit, have also lost favour because they might "lock women further into their caring role in the 'private' sphere of the family and out of the labour market and the 'public' sphere more generally".[78]

It is a particular worry to equal opportunities activists if women are part of couples, because they may continue to see income in terms of overall household resources, and not just as *their's*. This, plus the sheer dimensions of the costs entailed in providing for all mothers directly by the state, has meant that those who approach this option tend to withdraw after a brief reconnaissance.

Targeting the Marriage Allowance

As it is, the developing structure of support, like the weight of the recommendations behind it, is built specifically around the lone parent. It is an opting-in system for mothers who forgo or forsake marriage. It is accompanied by the withdrawal of support for couples or those in disfavoured circumstances, lest they might feel encouraged to combine resources and share out childrearing tasks. This has been nowhere more evident than in the concerted campaign to abolish the marriage allowance, supported by charitable and welfare organisations which are far from being regarded as radical. For example, The National Children's Home has stated that "a more appropriate mix of employment, training, child care, social security and maintenance arrangements must be developed to support lone parent families" while, in order for the tax system to reflect society's commitment to the well-being of children, "one possibility would be to phase out the married couples allowance and channel this money to families with children". Then, as more mothers are forced on to the labour market, "a network of affordable, local child care facilities will be required".[79] The National Children's Home does not question whether it is acceptable for the state to interfere through the tax system in the division of labour in the home, by forcing both spouses into paid work, and more single-wage couples below the benefit line.

The campaign scored a major victory with the Chancellor of the Exchequer's 1993 Budgets which cut back the level at which the marriage allowance could be claimed from the standard tax rates of 25 and 40 per cent to only 20 per cent in 1994-95. Describing the marriage allowance as an 'anomaly', the Chancellor proposed a further cut in 1995-96 to 15 per cent, and left little doubt that the long-term aim is to phase it out altogether. Coming on top of the freezing of the Allowance since 1991-92, these cuts have severely reduced its value (see p. 20) and made it less useful as a means of topping up Child Benefit, which now seems to be regarded as the only acceptable help which two-parent families can receive through the tax system.

Although some advocates of reform seem to imagine that the resources released by the abolition of the marriage allowance will be redistributed through an increased Child Benefit, they have already been ear marked by other influential lobbyists for more one-parent benefit. Allowances for lone parents are not open to

the hazards of mutual support. As noted earlier, The National
Council for One Parent Families has argued for the marriage
allowance to be retained for lone parents (as a lone-parent tax
allowance), while it is seen to be only proper to take it away
from couples.[80]

Of course, had the marriage allowance been converted into
Child Benefit, nothing would have been gained if, for example,
£2 of tax allowance converted into £2 of benefit, and much
would be lost if, for every £2 of tax allowance lost, only £1 of
benefit was substituted. But, whatever disappears from fathers'
wage packets, any 'increase' in Child Benefit "would be important in making many mothers less dependent upon male
partners for money to meet their children's needs".[81] Even if it
has not been cashed out, the reduction in the marriage allowance has not been unwelcome as it increases the discrepancy in
the taxation of one- and two-earner families. Families may not
gain, but, in feminist terms, they do not lose either if money is
removed from fathers, as this reduces men's capacity to create
'dependency' in women. It is particularly important that the tax
changes of the mid-1990s, will have the biggest impact in the
crucial middle-income group. Here it might have been possible
for one main earner to sustain a family, given that the allowance provided relief from the imposition of the higher rate tax
on solo incomes. That relief is now vanishing.

A bit of extra tax relief also provided some hope for men on
the margins who felt that, given some effort, there was a chance
that marriage and the rewards of work were not quite out of
their reach. Illustrating how the process of household formation
among poorer income groups is dictated by state systems, Bill
Jordan and colleagues describe how Ms Waveney, a single
mother, is living with Mr Trent and expecting his child. He is
on the brink of transforming himself into a new social identity,
from "carefree and pleasure-orientated single man" into a
"regular worker and provider of family income". Taxation is
crucial to the income and family strategy they will adopt. If they
declare themselves as living together, her benefits will be
adjusted and result in a substantial income loss. He earns
slightly above the Family Credit eligibility level and speculates
that, if he were in "married man's tax", he could take official
responsibility for his girlfriend as, with a little less disappearing
in taxation, it could boost his earnings by working harder. Their

decision turns upon the availability of an extra tax allowance, to transform them from a:

> ... single-parent claimant and leisure-orientated bachelor ... into a careful, responsible couple—he a regular worker doing overtime and seeking promotion, she the manager of the family's finances.[82]

It follows that the material and psychological impact of the withdrawal of this remaining measure of recognition for responsibilities in two-parent families will prevent such transitions. Their impracticality will be brought home by the way in which lone parents on Family Credit, who already enjoy more net income than two parents for the same effort, receive a substantial increase for childcare paid out of the penal taxation of two-parent families. Fathers' income "that could be used to enrich and to nourish their own children is being diverted, via taxes, to raise children of fatherless families".[83] The state is making it abundantly clear that it is not prepared to support a man's efforts to provide for a family and does not recognise his costs when his wife cares for his children. Rather, it is more willing to use the public assistance system to build up the wages of the lone mother and reimburse her for the expense of someone to look after the children, pay her one-parent benefit, give her maintenance disregards, and exemptions in local tax. Two-parent families, meanwhile, will have nothing to offset against their liabilities for mutual support.

At the same time, the pressure grows to expand these payments and provisions to lone parents. Increasingly, an enhanced One-parent Benefit, rather than a raised Child Benefit going to all parents, is advocated to reduce further the impact of means-tested benefit withdrawal, or the unemployment and poverty traps, for lone parents. This would be an adaptation of the Finer Committee's call for a Guaranteed Maintenance Allowance for all lone parents, with its special non-means-tested children's allowances (the adult means-tested part already being mainly achieved with higher rates of Income Support). It is suggested that the earnings disregard on Income Support should double for the lone parent, from a rate that is already treble that of a couple's. It could, of course, lead more lone parents to combine part-time work with Income Support as a long-term option. The answer to these problems is, in turn, to raise further the disregard for childcare or other work expenses that lone parents are entitled to if they extend their working hours and move onto Family Credit.

The Child Support Agency

To deal with fluctuations in maintenance payments and boost income, a system of advanced maintenance payments for every lone parent is regarded as the proper role of the Child Support Agency. The basic element is the payment of maintenance automatically by the state, which assumes the responsibility for collecting the money. Thus, if the absent parent cannot meet child support obligations, the custodial parent still receives a second income. Advanced maintenance schemes have been endorsed by the Council of Europe and are developing in a number of countries. In America, there is growing pressure for a federal programme.

The Child Support Agency was set up amidst consternation at the way in which the benefits bill was rising due to absent fathers' evasion of financial responsibility, although this should have been foreseen as a consequence of the 1984 'clean break' divorce legislation. On the face of it, it seems incongruous to abandon marriage as a lifelong commitment, and then to resurrect the husband as a perpetual provider. However, this is more apparent than real. In line with the withering away of marriage, the aim of the Child Support Agency is to ensure that maintenance rights are equalised between married and unmarried women. The legislation and regulations surrounding the Child Support Act make no reference to husbands, cohabitees or boyfriends, but simply refer to the responsibility of the natural parent.

Initially, the Child Support Agency met with feminist misgivings at the way in which the principle that absent parents should retain a responsibility for the maintenance of their children seemed to reinforce women's economic dependency on men. But its potential has soon been recognised as a way in which mothers could receive a guaranteed income from men through the intermediacy of the state. In other words, they can have the money without the man, whatever the circumstances leading to their condition.

In the meantime, the pressure is on to 'disregard' maintenance when lone parents are on Income Support and deal with the work disincentive problems by increasing the present disregards for those on Family Credit (all payments are, of course, disregarded outside the means-tested benefit system). There is little reason to question the optimism of the lone-parent lobby when it expects to get its way as easily here as it already has elsewhere. After all, does it not seem an eminently practical move? Would not fathers become more inclined to pay if their money did not offset the state's bill, and mothers—whose maintenance would otherwise be too much to qualify them for means-tested benefits—could now go on Income Support or Family Credit and receive all 'passport benefits' as well? Those lone parents who receive 'unofficial' subsidies from the child's father while drawing full benefits, and stand to lose from Child Support Agency activities, could be fully reconciled to the system if it endorsed the man's contributions as additional to benefits. This would legitimise what are essentially fraudulent claims. Moderate or low-income parents would receive substantial welfare payments in addition to the man's money so long as they did not marry.

While so many of the moves to increase the security and incomes of lone parents have been promoted as ways for the state to reduce its benefits bill, what is not taken into account is their propensity also to increase the movement into a far more expensive childrearing system from a comparatively cheap one. It may seem cheaper to pay women without evident male support than for the state to take responsibility for all mothers but, as this will disadvantage the married, the supply of eligible single mothers is bound to increase. The question is how much, particularly in terms of positive transfers, different arrangements for rearing children require; and whether or not the basic functions of childrearing can be covered by the family members or have to be transferred outside.

Unfortunately, moves to make the lone parent 'self-sufficient' usually involve shifting her from one heavily subsidised set of benefits and services to another. As Janet Bush says:

> Provide genuine part-time work opportunities and proper child care ... and many women would gladly not depend on the state.[84]

However, if this is not dependence on the state for wage subsidies and childrearing services, it is difficult to see what is. It has been self-evident through the ages that a mother on her own is not self-sufficient. Historically, raising children has devolved on groups, not individuals, with the progenitors, or those most directly involved, committed through marriage. It is very difficult for one person to devote the great effort and time required to raise a child while earning to support the family. The importance of the contribution of at least two people is magnified where the parents have low personal capacity and skills.

The Ascent of the Mother/Child Unit

Once the good father was defined both popularly and politically in terms of a good provider for his wife and children. Incentives and sanctions were so arranged that he received public approval for economically and emotionally supporting his wife and children. As succinctly explained by R.D. Day and W.C. Mackey, men do not obviously and immediately benefit more from fathering than by avoiding the parental role. As long as women are willing to cohabit or associate with men without marriage, then men are not sexually penalised for remaining single. If access to women is not contingent upon marriage and if the father's role is devalued, then non-marriage becomes attractive.[85]

Of course, a man may find being a parent sufficiently rewarding to modify economic preferences or, through ignorance or a taste for martyrdom, to do the best he can for his children while trying to absorb more taxes without complaint. His costs are three-fold. He saves the state the cost of providing for his own children, while helping to provide for other men's; he carries, unaided and unrecognised, the cost of a new generation, while funding the good life for the retired; finally, as an unemployed or low-paid man, he may see his children deprived relative to those of lone mothers. A man might well wonder why he "must exchange hard cash for more time spent caring for his children".[86] After all, his efforts do nothing to establish his right to live with and bring up his children, which is only enjoyed at the mother's discretion. As a reforming Law Commissioner puts it, "The radical improvements made and still proposed in the remedies available for dependent wives have greatly reduced the legal attractions of marriage for men".[87] While there is much publicity for the plight of the single mother, there is none for the problems of the married father supporting his own children.[88] Instead, it is widely conveyed that his presence is oppressive and unnecessary.

Uncertain economic prospects mean that family formation problems are likely to get worse anyway. However, when this is coupled with a strongly deterrent tax and benefit structure, more and more men will have increasingly reduced incentives to get married. As the disincentives to assume the role of father increase, so more and more men will avoid it. We will witness the increasing destruction of the family, not only for low income communities, but further up the social scale as well. Taxation must keep on rising to pay both for an ageing population and growing numbers of lone mothers, particularly as the benefits system accelerates social security spending by allowing businesses to replace full-time jobs with part-time work on a mass scale.

As taxes help to make it progressively more difficult for any wife to stay out of the workforce, the numbers of children born to married mothers will continue to fall. Accordingly, the percentage of all children born to unwed mothers is predicted to go on rising at an exponential rate. In the ongoing contest between two reproductive strategies, the "direction of the social dynamic is towards fewer traditional families and more woman-state-child families".[89] Not only Day and Mackey in America, but a less apprehensive Duncan J. Dormor in Britain, see the advent of a matrilineal system under which:

> ... more people will have a succession of relationships with different partners ... If this trend continues the only continuing relationship a child may have will be with its mother.[90]

Under such a system, men become peripheral to family life. Current trends—as well as current plans—make this a realistic possibility.

All human societies have controlled reproduction by manipulating the conditions in which an individual can, or cannot, have offspring. Groups ensure their survival and success by limiting procreation to those adults expected to have the best chance of providing for their children. This has been brought about by restricting marriage, whether by dowry, brideprice, military service or numerous other mechanisms. The Western system largely developed on the basis of attaining a certain living standard in an independent household. These conditions must be obtainable by sufficient numbers if a viable population is to be sustained, unless the criteria for reproduction change. To use a natural analogy: birds need territory to breed, but there are no breeding territories if the habitat is eroded or destroyed. What is novel about the present situation is the destruction of marriage as the habitat for human procreation.

Whether the woman/child unit can compete with the man/woman/child family in terms of success in childrearing, is another matter. If lone parents have greater difficulties in many respects, this raises the further question of how far it is possible to provide supplements or substitutes on top of the financial package to enable one person to cover all childrearing functions. The ascent of the mother/child unit has been accompanied by arguments for help and supports to make these 'fully-functional' as much as 'self-sufficient'. The mandate for any necessary public provision is the Children Act 1989. This represents a move away from provision of support services as a reactive measure, towards a proactive programme of support for children in need, in which the task of local authorities is to develop coherent strategies of support. While ostensibly combining machinery for helping children at risk with the aim of keeping families together, this might equally be described as a policy founded on the demise of the family as the place for the care of children and its replacement by the state.

5

Same Incomes, Same Outcomes?

Summary: *The family based on marriage has always been recognised as the mechanism for socialising the next generation. Advocates of 'new family forms' argue that children of lone parents or remarried parents do as well as those brought up by both biological parents, but extensive research findings refute this claim. Children of non-traditional families have higher rates of mortality and morbidity; are more at risk of abuse; more likely to become delinquent and go into care and more likely to become involved in crime. This is sometimes countered by claims that the poverty of lone parents accounts for the different outcomes, but research which controls for income shows that this is not the case. With the decline of marriage the social network which sets and maintains standards of acceptable behaviour in a community fragments. Not only do large numbers of fatherless youths represent a high risk factor for crime in an area; the effect on the men who are unattached to any family is serious. Marriage and parenthood have traditionally been the route through which delinquent youths become responsible citizens—a route which will be increasingly closed off.*

Just a Matter of Economics?

WE HAVE become accustomed over recent years to having the two-parent, conjugal family represented as inherently problematic or flawed, as well as dismissed and ridiculed as a ludicrous charade that is on the way out. There is no precise equivalent to this when it comes to lone parenthood, which is rather seen as a successor compatible with women's growing independence. But this reversal of the customary reputations of the family and the unmarried woman with children since the 1960s is without historical or cultural precedent. Bronislaw Malinowski, the outstanding founder of modern anthropology, could confidently assert earlier in this century, that:

> I know of no single instance in anthropological literature of a
> community where illegitimate children, that is children of

113

unmarried girls, would enjoy the same social treatment and have the same social status as legitimate ones.

The 'necessity for imposing the bond of marriage' was:

> ... practically and theoretically due to the fact that a father has to be made to look after his children. An illegitimate child has, as a rule, no chance of receiving the same care from its natural father as a legitimate one and the latter is cared for to a large extent because it is the father's duty.[1]

The widow woman has always been the object of sympathy and charity, precisely in awareness of the precariousness of young life in the absence of a father's support. Her position was involuntary. In contrast, women who might perhaps have avoided getting in a similar predicament could expect to bring down much wrath on their heads. Individual mothers and infants suffered, but the group could not have dealt with a widespread problem of minimally attached children. No society could have survived without making sure its children were raised by parents who took responsibility for them; and none ever felt that it could take over this responsibility.

When doubts are intermittently raised today about the ability of one person to cope adequately with childrearing they provoke much outrage and denial. It is significant that the question of whether outcomes for the children of lone parents are the same as those from two-parent families should matter so much. Human beings depend upon a lengthy education process to equip each generation with the skills, knowledge and possessions essential for the survival and success of individuals and society. However, traditionally it was taken for granted that families were the basis of social cohesion and that it was vital to have a complete set of kin relations, or affiliations that spanned both sexes, across and down generations. These ties told you who you were, gave you your place in the world and were the basis of your inheritance from it. As David W. Murray describes:

> Legitimacy is nothing more nor less than the orderly transfer of social meaning across the generations. Remember that children are the ultimate illegal aliens. They are undocumented immigrants to our world, who must be socialised and invested with identity, a culture and an estate. By conferring legitimacy marriage keeps this process from becoming chaos.

In particular:

Traditional society is composed of only two kinds of people—relatives and strangers. The social world centres around kinship identities, and relatives are those with whom you work, worship, ally, sleep, play, and die. Kinsmen bear you, nurse you in illness, initiate you into adulthood, protect you from injustice, and bury you into the order of the ancestors.[2]

It is indicative of the radical challenge to the family that it is now being asked to justify itself in bald, utilitarian terms without reference to these profound cultural considerations. It seems to be assumed that if only the outcomes of different types of relationships could be made equal, in terms of children's education and health, for example, then any residual case for the family would collapse. In the post counter culture landscape, there would seem to be no rationale left for something which restricts people's right to conduct their sex lives as they please. If the practical consequences for children are removed what, asks Polly Toynbee, does moral disquiet over the demise of marriage mean apart from "a desire to keep people in their proper place, and maybe an underlying fear of freedom"?[3] The wish for two parents is just something "people ideally want for themselves" blown up into a belief that children need fathers, when it does not represent the desire to "put women back into the home under the authority of men", according to Sue Slipman, director of the National Council for One Parent Families.[4]

There has been no shortage of voices emphasising that lone parenthood provides a perfectly salutary environment for child rearing. If some insist that lone parenthood means superior parenting, this follows from claims that child abuse, like female subjugation, are products of the male-dominated conjugal family. "There is more abuse of children in a traditional family where there is a man", is the authoritative verdict of popular agony aunt Claire Rayner. "To assume that having two parents together is necessarily better is one of the fantasies".[5] And, if men contribute little or nothing that is positive to a home, their absence may even be seen as a gain for the child, in terms of more attention from a mother who has no husband to take up her time. Moreover:

> ... from the point of view of the child—the experience of being brought up by a lone parent can include sensations of relief, of simplicity; and an experience of personal, top-quality attention which may otherwise not have been their lot.[6]

This all flies in the face of a considerable body of evidence suggesting that children who grow up with both original parents are, on the whole, better off than children living with single parents and in stepfamilies, whether in terms of health, mortality, school performance, intellectual development, behavioural and emotional problems, law-breaking, leaving home, employment, drug taking, early pregnancy and other measures. Indeed, David Poponoe, sociologist of the family, describes how "in three decades of work, I know of few other bodies of data in which the weight of evidence is so decisively one side of the issue".[7] But studies showing how children's well-being is strongly associated with family structure are apt to be ignored or played down and those instances highlighted where differences in the performance of children from various types of homes were not picked up or the results are ambiguous. Simultaneously, any differences are attributed to economic factors, or lone-parent poverty. Anna Coote, Harriet Harman and Patricia Hewitt insist that:

> There is little evidence to support the assertion that lone parenthood—or lone motherhood—is *itself* a direct cause of under-achievement of children, juvenile delinquency, crime or general social disintegration.[8]

and that:

> While it is possible to show differences between children of lone-parent and two-parent families, in terms of their emotional and educational development, the weight of evidence suggests that these differences are due to the material circumstances of the families in question.[9]

If, indeed, it can be shown "that all of the effects of single parenthood are caused by the economic circumstances of single mothers, that is another way of saying that single parenthood in and of itself has no effect on the next generation".[10] Had lone parents enough money then their children would be generally as competent, healthy, qualified and law-abiding as those from two-parent families, according to this view.

Iron Laws and Statistical Probabilities

The argument often becomes a methodological one. Claims that children growing up with lone parents may do less well than those with married couples are simultaneously condemned for dooming, or sentencing, all children in one category to do badly *and*, at the same time, for being misleading, because the adverse effect is not present in 100 per cent of cases. But in the social and behavioural sciences, or medical epidemiology, researchers are not looking for strict exceptionless laws, as in physics, but probabilities. This means something which occurs at a significantly higher rate in one group compared to another, and whose distribution is not due to accident or chance. It is no sign of failure that we do not know who precisely is going to be adversely affected, although further comparative investigations could narrow this down. We know that 100 per cent of smokers are not going to get lung cancer, only a minority, and we cannot say who these will be, but this does not make smoking any less a significant risk factor in populations. To dismiss findings because there are exceptions is to demand impossible standards that would abolish social and medical investigation altogether.

Findings are group averages. Measures of the frequency of any characteristic in different groups greatly overlap and there is no problem showing good results at the best end of the worst distribution, and bad results at the worst end of the best distribution. It is easy to make the:

> ... very obvious contrast ... between children who grow up in a loving one-parent family and children who grow up in two-parent families and are neglected or abused.[11]

If a government-funded body goes to the trouble to produce reports simply to tell us that "Neither family disruption nor lone parenthood are inevitably associated with poorer outcomes for children compared with those in intact families",[12] or that the "assumption that two parents are automatically a better safeguard against delinquency is not ... supported by the evidence",[13] these are hardly revelations or discoveries. They do not invalidate possible evidence that both situations may not produce the same proportions of good and bad effects.

This is an area where far more stringent (or impossible) standards of proof are expected, and adverse findings tend to be minimised, compared to many of those which, for example, deal with pollutants, diet or disease. It supposedly puts the gravity of the problem into perspective if illegitimate children have overall reading scores close to those of children from intact homes of manual workers.[14] Yet, if the reading ages of increasing numbers of children move towards the manual working-class level with changes in childrearing, this will be reflected in national educational performance. Similarly, even if an analysis suggesting that delinquent behaviour is 10 per cent to 15 per cent more prevalent for children without their two natural parents is to be preferred over others,[15] it will still make quite a difference to overall predation rates in a community if large numbers of children are moving into higher risk groups.

However, Ann Hagell and Tim Newburn's recent Policy Studies Institute study of persistent young offenders presents a far more serious situation. Here, 15 of the 74 re-offenders successfully interviewed were living with neither parent, five with their fathers only, 32 with their mothers only and 22 living with what are described as two parents, but including step-parents, mother's boyfriends and grandparents. As if it were possible, the degree of family disruption in the lives of persistent young offenders is said to be under-represented, since those with the most chaotic lives are so difficult for interviewers to find (156 out of an original sample of 251 were uncontactable or untraced).[16]

Of course, it is right to object that, in this study, we are reading backwards. What we do not know is how many young people with backgrounds as chaotic as the re-offenders *do not get* into persistent trouble, although it would be surprising if such disruptive backgrounds were not more common among the seriously delinquent than the law-abiding. The Cambridge Study of Delinquent Development, the main British study to date of criminal careers, showed that delinquents were not only more likely to be born illegitimate, but there was a doubling of the risk of delinquency where homes were broken by divorce.[17] In the longitudinal Oregon Youth Study boys who had been through divorce by the age of 10 were more likely to be anti-social. This was especially marked where they had step-fathers, so that their chances of arrest were double those of children living with both biological parents.[18] Data from the National Child Development Study, the main longitudinal study of child development in Britain is frequently referred to in reviews of the outcomes for children of different backgrounds. What is likely to be missing is the finding from the 16-year-old follow up that, while eight per cent of boys with both natural parents had been to court at some time, the figure was 16 per cent for those with lone mothers and 19 per cent for boys with step-fathers. Those who had dealings with police or probation officers were respectively nine per cent, 17 per cent and 20 per cent.[19]

In social science there is no problem in finding ambiguous studies or ones contrary to the rest, but the significant unit of research is the progressive series of studies and the convergence of results. The trouble is that those who are more interested in special pleading than genuine enquiry have a habit of citing exceptions to the rule as *the* rule. A study often used to clinch the matter is one for the Home Office in 1985 on Parental Supervision and Delinquency.[20] This found no differences for self-reported delinquency in the previous 12 months on the part of teenagers from one- and two-parent families. But then it also failed to find any relationship between delinquency and any measure of a family's economic or social difficulty or stress, including large family and rough neighbourhood, which have been correlated with law-breaking elsewhere. Furthermore, living arrangements were recorded at the time of interview, not over time, and did not distinguish between widowhood and lone parenthood as a result of other causes, or between two-parent families with original parents from those with step-parents. In other studies these distinctions are important for outcomes. What it did find, however, was that delinquency was strongly associated with a lack of involvement or positive feelings between fathers and teenagers.

Willing the Worst?

All this, however, does not stop the claim that "one sure way to stunt the healthy development of children growing up in one-parent or reconstituted families is to give them the impression that their families are incomplete or deviant".[21] Delinquency, according to this view, is the self-fulfilling prophecy of a labelling process. If the problems of children of lone parents can be boiled down to a lack of self-esteem due to prejudice and negative expectations, then the social disapproval of single mothers from which these stem is attributed to "a lack of faith in women's capacity for executive leadership".[22] Once we aid in the empowerment of the mother-headed family, the promise is that any disadvantage which their children suffer will evaporate.

An extension of this argument is that it is the existence or social support for the two-parent family, marriage or a family structure which involves the affiliation of men to particular children, which is to blame. Outcomes would not be comparatively unfavourable to lone mothers if societies had organised procreation so that the mother carried out all the functions of childrearing herself, or these functions were devolved, on her behalf, to specialist agencies. Similarly:

> ... it is society's failure to develop appropriate norms governing stepfamily relationships that poses the greatest obstacle to their successful functioning. It is a disturbing fact that while, in practice, diversity of family forms has always existed, at the ideological level the 'nuclear family' of two married parents and their biological children remains the only type which receives full recognition and endorsement. ...
>
> Until we stop trying to force stepfamilies into the normative framework which has relevance only for the 'biological' nuclear family we will not achieve the flexibility of values that such families need in order to fulfill their childrearing, socialising role.[23]

Such 'flexibility' presumably means the 'full recognition and endorsement' of serial unions, and the rightfulness of adults with children moving in or out of 'partnerships' as inclined. It implies the obliteration of notions of permanency or extended commitment for *all* adults with children. After all, nuclear families and stepfamilies do not constitute separate populations who can have different rules.

Obviously, doubts or questions of whether children do better in some circumstances compared to others are often perceived as a challenge to the validity of new 'family forms'. But neither the demographic prevalence of the conjugal, nuclear family, nor the degree to which it is acclaimed or execrated as an ideal, alters the *fact* that family structures may differ in the opportunities they extend to growing children. Raising a child is difficult enough under any circumstances, and it is not unreasonable to suppose that it might be more prone to problems when someone tries to do it alone. People are quite capable of appreciating that, whether by accident or choice, their condition may not be ideal, or they may not be best placed to achieve certain ends. Moreover, policy-makers need to know what is required in terms of special services to make any 'family lifestyle' fully 'operational'. It may not always be possible to get some kinds of home to function as well as others, or it may demand more or different resources and facilities. We therefore need to consider both the question of how much of the variation in the outcomes for children from different family backgrounds is due to economic conditions, as well as how far it might be possible to reduce or remove, any differences and what this could involve.

More Input, Same Output?

Here it is necessary to draw attention to a distinction usually not made. This is whether the disadvantages of children of lone parents *vis-à-vis* those of two parents are due to differences in their economic status so that, were they *in a comparable financial position*, outcomes would also be equal, or whether *there are differences in outcome even at comparative economic positions*, which could still nonetheless be overcome with extra resources. While they are inclined to roll the two up together, it often seems that lone-parent apologists are talking about the latter. This undermines the claim that differences only reflect financial inequality. It means that, to equalise outcomes, the mother-child unit requires a complex of remedial provisions, or substitutes for what the two parent family is more likely to supply as a matter of course.

It is true that children reared in poverty are more likely to enter school with growth deficits and learning difficulties, just as money is a primary cause of tension and disputes in families. Conflict induced or exacerbated by poverty and financial hardship can develop into emotional and behavioural problems in the children. However, where this leads to the formation of lone-parent households, conditions may be created in which children are *more vulnerable all the time*.[24] Such connections are represented on a macro, or social, level, in the analyses of those like Robert Sampson, who shows that unemployment, low per capita income and poverty relate to delinquency, crime and violence indirectly through family breakdown, unmarried births and female headed households.

It might seem simpler to give more encouragement to two-parent families as a means of reducing demand for expensive and uncertain remedial measures. However, as it is hard to promote something without seeming to approve of it, this would be difficult to reconcile with the "need to avoid moral judgements about the *rightness* of two-parent family life".[25] And, whatever difficulties are envisaged in getting the mother-child unit 'fully-functional', the alternative is rejected as investment in the 'family system of the past'. Indeed, it is "nostalgia for the family", according to Patricia Hewitt and Penelope Leach, which "is preventing us from getting to grips with the task of making today's families, in all their infinite variety, work".[26] What is not considered is that, if some family structures cannot be made to work as well as others, a system which makes a disproportionate amount of provision for the less efficient may be furthering conditions of relatively greater risk to children, as well as employing national resources in the least cost effective way.

Questions of Life and Death

The differences which exist between children of various backgrounds are illustrated dramatically by the death tables. The infant mortality rate for babies born outside marriage and registered by the mother alone now stands 80 per cent higher than that of babies born within marriage. Children are also likely to die at a higher rate. This is seen with the National Child Development Study (based on a mass sample of children born in 1958) in which 52 per 1,000 of the children born out-of-wedlock were dead by the age of seven as against 36 per 1,000 for those with fathers, after allowing for birthweight and maternal class and age.[27]

A recent study in Finland found perinatal deaths, low birthrate, and premature infants more common among single than married mothers (after adjusting for maternal age, education, smoking and other factors).[28] A study of data collected from the Jamaican Fertility Survey reveals a clear gradient for the impact of sexual status on infant mortality, where the risk was highest for women with no relationship to any particular man and lowest for the married, being intermediate for cohabiting women and those with a regular 'visiting' man.[29] However, when other variables known to affect infant mortality, like the years of schooling, education and age of the mother, or the birth order of the child, were taken into consideration, the risk of experiencing an infant death set marriage even more sharply apart from the other types of union.

Absence of the father is among the factors which exacerbate the increased risk of infant mortality, morbidity and behavioural problems for the children of teenage mothers. Explanations in terms of stigma and lack of resources are difficult to square with evidence, like that provided by Trevor Lummis from East Anglian fishing communities in the nineteenth and early twentieth centuries. Here the number of child deaths in two-parent families where the father was absent from home for long periods because of his work were double those where he did not have to travel.[30]

If anything, the exclusion from present class-based analyses of mortality of children when a parent is classed as 'unoccupied' (rather than unemployed), and who consist largely (89 per cent) of single mothers on social security benefits, has resulted in a misleading rosy picture of the health status of the children of British lone parents. The death rate for children aged 0-15 years for such 'unoccupied' parents is 42 per cent worse than that for class V, which covers the lowest income group, including many unemployed and those two-parent families living below the Income Support line and three times worse than that for children in class I. Accidents and injuries account for nearly 60 per cent of deaths, twice the proportion found in the rest of the population.[31]

The contribution that fathers make to reduced mortality and morbidity is not simply a matter of the way in which two parents can supplement each other, and each can compensate or help to make up for any of the deficiencies of the other. There are indirect effects of quite impressive scope and consequences which demonstrate how being a group involves a qualitative, as well as a quantitative, difference. Satisfaction in the marital relationship is associated with good parenting and clearly makes a critical contribution to the trajectory of the mother-child relationship and the child's development. From the earliest days, the father's support for the mother increases her effectiveness and sensitivity in the care and feeding of her infant, as well as enhancing and reinforcing her relationship with the child and her role as a parent. New parents are even more likely to examine and tend to their babies when their partners are present.[32]

Because of this, there is reason to suspect that children born outside marriage cannot be expected to be as healthy as children born in wedlock. Furthermore, there is a question-mark over the extent to which negative implications can be overcome by government policies designed to equalise the life chances of children from different backgrounds. It may be possible to provide more medical and welfare services, but it is difficult to

see how these can entirely compensate for the absence of a
positive, continuous domestic relationship with someone with an
equal, or even greater, interest in a child's welfare.

The health of the mother also has more far-reaching implications for the child of a lone parent than one with two parents.
If she dies, the child becomes a no-parent child. The immediate
risks are illustrated by the growing number of instances where
small children have been found to have spent lengthy periods
shut in with the bodies of their mothers. Their longer-term
welfare will lie with professional social services in a way that
has not traditionally been the case on parental death, since there
is a widow, or widower, to carry on.

The extended family is also less likely to be able to help,
since its numbers are often depleted by lone parenthood, particularly where the natural father never had, or has lost, contact
with his children. Marriage is a device that "extends to us a
social security network of obligated kin" or social capital.
Without it, few people are tied in a committed and socially
sanctioned way to the obligation of support. As lone parenthood
passes through more than one generation, the result is "an
almost exponential collapse of the number of supporting relatives".[33] The first generation lone-parent child is likely to lack
one set of grandparents, uncles and aunts and, in the second
generation, there will be only one grandmother. Parents who
experience marital breakdown are less likely to feel supported by
relatives compared with intact families. Children are also more
likely to lose touch with grandparents and other important
relatives after experiencing family transitions. This loss of
contact extends to former step-parents, half-brothers and half-
sisters.[34]

Since the lone-parent child is critically dependent upon the
viability of one adult, that person's mental or physical illness
can devastate the home in ways which would be less likely were
there two parents. Unfortunately, lone mothers also have a
three-fold disadvantage when it comes to health: they are
women, parents and not married. Higher levels of stress are
associated with parental status, for both mothers and fathers,
and especially employed women with young children. Women
have more depression and psychiatric symptoms than men, but
the single and divorced of both sexes have higher death rates at
all ages than the married, and high consulting levels for

infectious and respiratory disease, mental disorders and accidents. Admissions to mental hospitals are far higher for single and divorced women, and studies of depression and psychological well-being all show lone mothers using more mental health services than married mothers or childless women.[35]

Abusive Relations

Child homicide and abuse rates are higher in developed nations where rates of births to teenagers, divorce, illegitimacy and the proportions of non-intact families are higher.[36] This is not surprising considering that children from backgrounds of family disruption comprise a majority of the victims of all major forms of active child abuse, physical, emotional and sexual, and a majority of victims of neglect, despite being greatly outnumbered in the population by children from intact two-parent homes. Only 40 per cent of children on the NSPCC's child protection registers in the 1980s lived with both their natural parents at the time of abuse, while most of the other 60 per cent lived with either their mother alone or their mother and her 'boyfriend' or other 'father-substitute'.[37]

If lone mothers themselves are more likely to abuse or neglect children compared with married women, we might surmise that, as with any enterprise, including childrearing, standards are maintained, performance improved and excesses checked through the expectations and responses of other people. Those on their own do not receive the feedback which encourages and tells them that their efforts are right and worthwhile, and neither are they policed and corrected by another concerned parent. In turn, parents who have themselves been abused or spent part of their childhood in care are far less likely to repeat a pattern of parental inadequacy if they have a supportive spouse from a 'normal' background. When they parent alone, this chance of rehabilitation is removed and the likelihood is that more problems are added to, than withdrawn from, the cycle of disadvantage.[38]

Paternal absenteeism is often combined with the presence of unrelated males in the home, where the mother may associate, on a regular or intermittent basis, with one or a succession of men. Yet a man with no blood ties to the children is more likely to kill or ill-treat them than the biological father, and the risk from a man without either a blood or legal tie to the children in the household (i.e. the boyfriend, rather than stepfather) is greatest of all. Marriage increases commitment to the father role even in men who are not the biological fathers of the children in the household, partly, no doubt, because it brings into play the incest taboo as an aspect of the imperative to suspend self-gratification in the interests of others.[39] Examination of court records between 1982 and 1988 has shown a risk factor for abuse 20 times greater when the natural parents were not married compared with when they were. In turn, the risk of abuse for children whose mothers were cohabiting was five and a half times greater than for children with step-fathers.[40]

However, in reality as in folklore, step-relationships are far more conflictual and dangerous than the corresponding genetic relationships. Child abuse specialists Martin Daly and Margo Wilson claim that: "The presence of a step parent is the best epidemiological predictor of child abuse risk yet discovered".[41] Their analysis of American records revealed that children under three incurred about seven times higher rates of 'validated' sublethal physical abuse in step-parent homes than in two-genetic-parent homes. In subsequent Canadian studies they found that toddlers living in step-households were about 40 times more likely to become registered victims of severe physical abuse than their two-genetic-parent counterparts, and twice as likely to be murdered. This does not just occur in developed societies. Among foraging South American tribes, 43 per cent of children raised by a mother and stepfather die before their fifteenth birthday, compared to only 19 per cent of those raised by two genetic parents. Historical demographic analysis shows similar results in Europe.[42] All this evidence should be viewed in the context of a number of studies which show as high or higher rates of delinquency, early home leaving and behavioural problems for children in stepfather families, as for those of lone parents.

As parental care is always costly in terms of personal resources, some people may be less willing to use up time and money which might otherwise be spent on their own genetic children by incurring major costs on unrelated young. Even if step-parents were relieved of any calls which unrelated children might make on their time and income, there still remains the problem that offspring from a previous union may not only compete for the mother's attention, but militate against her having more children by subsequent consorts. In the National

Child Development Study stepfathers were considerably less interested in children's school progress than were fathers in unbroken families. Almost twice as many (33 per cent to 18 per cent) were rated as showing little or no interest and only 24 per cent, compared to 45 per cent of natural fathers, were very interested, whatever their social class. Moreover, if single or divorced mothers were comparatively uninterested in their children, the same went for remarried mothers, especially when they had sons. (Only 24 per cent were very interested, compared to 43 per cent of mothers in unbroken families.) Stepfather families also contained the highest proportion who wanted their children to leave school at the earliest possible opportunity, and had the lowest aspirations when it came to jobs. Social class made no difference in the case of boys.[43]

No doubt there are higher risks to children associated with certain backgrounds or parental characteristics where there is less generous welfare spending.[44] This may reduce abuse as well as health risks by countering lone parents' lack of social support and isolation, and by providing child protection services. But it is difficult to see how the risk-enhancing effects of some conditions can be entirely counteracted by surveillance and other social and economic resources supplied by public bodies. Moreover, large numbers of lone parents may raise the overall risks of violence by weakening the networks of informal support and control in a community as a whole.

Submissions to the Australian Burdekin report on homeless children from numerous refuges and counts in different states revealed that between three-quarters and nearly 100 per cent of these youngsters were from step-families or lone-parent households.[45] According to British data from the National Child Development Study, the odds are that a young man from a step-family or with a lone parent will leave home for negative reasons at a rate three to six times higher than if he had an intact family.[46] The question arises of whether local authorities can keep pace with the housing demand created by divorce, lone parenthood and strained step relations, as envisaged in the 1989 Children Act. This is a situation where supply is likely to create or contribute to its own demand. A 'needs led' approach, with anything but the most discriminating selection of cases for assistance, could lead to the expectation of accommodation almost as a matter of course. Lone mothers have come to occupy a large proportion of available public housing within a very short time, and it is easy to envisage a similar expansion for young single men.

As a 'looked after child' the Children Act emphasises how a teenager housed by a local authority is entitled to a wide range of support services, including maintenance in kind or even cash. It is envisaged that 'adolescent teams' of special social workers and members of voluntary bodies could help with everything from practical skills to building social and sexual relationships. It is not clear whether surrogate parenting or 'structured support programmes for young people in the community' are meant, for example, to reverse the tendency of youngsters from disrupted families to leave school at the minimum age.[47]

Use of Care Placements

Abuse, neglect, abandonment, serious delinquencies, the death or ill health of parents, or their incapacity to cope, make children candidates for care proceedings. Those who have been in care are heavily represented among homeless and penal populations, so that 38 per cent of those aged between 17 and 20 held in custody in 1991 had experience of care before 16. It would be mistaken to attribute such outcomes simply to care itself.[48] Deficiencies in performance exist before children are likely to spend time in institutions or foster homes, and are owed as much to factors like a lack of parental attention, conflict and stress.[49]

Receptions into care are not randomly distributed among children from different home backgrounds, or proportional to percentages of lone parents and two-parent families in the population. In their survey of the backgrounds of 2,500 children entering local authority care, Andrew Bebbington and John Miles[50] found that three out of four had lone parents. A half also came from poor neighbourhoods and three-quarters of their families relied on Income Support. We may be dealing with an economically badly off population, but this does not explain the preponderance of lone-parent children in care, or why, as Peter Marsh found, only 18 per cent of children who were 'volunteered' or surrendered to the care system, had two natural parents. It seems that, particularly at the poorest levels, a resident father is a significant barrier to the children being taken or received into care.[51]

Since many parents of children at imminent risk of care lack positive support with the burden of raising children, the idea is that more family centres, professional family aides and therapists to provide intensive help in the home with housework, budgeting, emotional support and assistance with parenting, might be more cost effective as well as less disruptive if they forestall receptions into care.[52] Even so, just how feasible is it to provide coverage with such complex and expensive preventative schemes, if a growing proportion of children are brought up in conditions where the use of care is more common?

The Quality of Research

The figures which we have been examining bear out only too well the observation of Sara McLanahan (foremost American researcher on the subject) that, while a decade ago the prevailing view that single motherhood or divorce had no harmful effects on children might just have been permissible, recent research is less optimistic and the problem is more serious than conventional wisdom has deemed it to be.[53] In Britain Jack Dominian and colleagues at the marital research body One Plus One insist that, while single parents may often have economic difficulties, "it is naïve to see the problems of such families in terms of poverty alone" and to think that opportunity can be equalised purely by money.[54]

Into the 1960s, much work purporting to describe the pathologies of children from broken homes was based on highly selective samples (such as those in therapy for psychological disorders or delinquents in custody); used subjective, interpretative and impressionistic observations (often inspired by psychoanalysis), and had poor controls, if any. By the 1970s, researchers were demonstrating how work on fatherless families contained serious methodological faults and, in particular, that no account was taken of differences in socio-economic status. However, despite their insistence "that father absence *did* have some negative consequences for children", the criticism "was taken by many as evidence that differences between one and two-parent families were minimal or due entirely to income differences".[55]

Since the early 1980s many American studies based on large, nationally representative surveys have incorporated longitudinal designs which follow children from different backgrounds into adulthood. These use standardised measures and the researchers have repeated these studies with more than one data set, using various and sophisticated statistical techniques to test for possible connections between variables.

> The new research indicates that children who grow up in mother-only families are disadvantaged not only during childhood or immediately after their parents' marital disruption, but during adolescence and young adulthood as well. Moreover, the negative consequences associated with family structure extend across a wide range of socio-economic outcomes.[56]

This has happened against a background of rising divorce and out-of-wedlock births. As more children experience divorce or live with one parent, so the stigma is reduced. This might have been predicted to ameliorate any unpleasant effects, but even Louie Burghes, who is anxious to put the most optimistic construction on the evidence, concedes that:

> ... the lessons from the United States ... are not encouraging. Their experience of a higher divorce rate over a longer period of time has not resulted in improving outcomes for children.[57]

How Much Difference Does Money Make?

While it is often suggested that researchers are still so stupid as to quite overlook matters of economics, the sophistication of some work goes so far as to give us some idea of the proportion of any result that could be attributed to financial factors. Thus Sara McLanahan calculated, for example, that income accounted for between 40 per cent to 50 per cent of the difference in high school drop-out rates between children from mother-only and two-parent families in one of her American studies.[58] Analysis of three longitudinal surveys showed how family income accounted for between 13 per cent and 50 per cent of the relationships between growing up with a lone mother and becoming a single parent in adulthood, depending on which sample was used, and whether one looked at blacks, whites or Hispanics.[59] Her own analysis of the data from the Panel Study of Income Dynamics showed how differences in income accounted for up to 25 per cent of the cycle of lone parenthood (and so not for 75 per cent). Thus, between 50 per cent and 87 per cent of the difference is unexplained by economic factors.[60]

Some studies, like William Aquilino's investigation of early home leaving in America (based on the 1988 National Survey of

Families and Households), showed no relationship between the tendency of children in non-intact families to seek early independence and to be less likely to attend higher education, and the parents' economic status.[61] Similarly, in Sanford M. Dornbusch and colleagues' work on the control of adolescents, measures of social class or parental income and education did not affect the consistent relationship between mother-only households and higher rates of deviance.[62] In Sheila Fitzgerald Krein's and Andrea H. Beller's study, using the National Longitudinal Survey of Labor Market Experience, the longer the time spent with a lone parent, the greater the reduction in educational attainment. Controlling for income did not noticeably reduce its significantly adverse effect on men—only women. And, if living with a lone parent had the greatest negative impact in the pre-school years, income had no effect on this timing.[63]

If the educational attainment, or behaviour, of the children of lone parents is affected by their income then, by the same token, we must expect the same to hold for children from two-parent families at an equivalent financial level. If it is only a matter of economics, then outcomes should be equal for those in the same economic position.

This tends not to be the case. Sheppard Kellam and colleagues followed hundreds of poor, black boys in a depressed neighbourhood of Chicago for ten years. Those who had grown up in mother-only families reported more delinquencies than those who had grown up in families with multiple adults, especially fathers, regardless of any income differences that there were.[64] On a national scale, the 1988 National Health Interview Survey on Child Health, involving 17,110 children aged 17 or under, found that of behaviour problems, anti-social behaviour, anxiety and depression, headstrong behaviour, hyperactivity, dependency, peer conflict or social withdrawal were higher at lower income levels, and then tended to diminish up the income scale for children in all circumstances. However, within income bands, which start at a household income under US$10,000 per annum and go up to US$50,000 and over, the differences between children from different family types persist. Table 5.1 (p. 160), showing mean scores for behavioural problems, is typical.[65]

The Human Input

Any suggestions that income is the only factor entailed in educational under-performance or delinquency contradicts the observation that the more attention children receive from involved adults, the better the outcome. The higher the ratio of children to adults the more extenuated parental attention is likely to be, and this probably accounts for the frequent finding that children from large families in all classes do not do so well educationally compared to those from smaller families.

Parental investment in children depends upon time and money. The outcome is affected by parental ability to combine these resources for producing achievement, and this will depend upon parental skills, education and intelligence. In the survey of 13,135 British five-year-olds for the Child Health and Education Study it was found that children of lone parents and those from families with five or more children had significantly poorer vocabulary and, by inference, linguistic ability, compared to those from two-parent and smaller families. Children with the poorest scores lived with grandparents and in foster homes and were likely to have come from disrupted backgrounds.[66]

Where one parent is absent he cannot be spending time with the children, and this may also reduce the availability of the mother because she has to do many tasks performed by fathers in two-parent homes. Not only is one parent missing, but the remaining parent may spend less time on primary child-care activities, with comparatively less affection, supervision, and attention and a comparative lack of household order, activities and predictable *régimes*. The mother's social and sex life, courtship and boyfriends may compete for attention with the children, and her reference points are more likely to shift away from the home. Lower levels of parental involvement and supervision, which are found more frequently in mother-only homes, affect everything from help with homework to the monitoring of adolescents' social activities.[67] These give rise to observations that lone mothers have less input into their children's decisions than married parents and, in consequence, adolescents may be more susceptible to peer pressure.[68]

Instead, paternal absenteeism may mean generally lower levels of contact between adults and children, so that family life is more sparse and perfunctory. It is possible to speak of a centrifugal, rather than a centripetal, process—pulling family members apart, rather than drawing them together at home. This is illustrated by a longitudinal, comparative study of the educational and vocational development of different ethnic groups in the Midlands, which showed a cumulative deficit for West Indians, compared to white and Indian children on reading, IQ and verbal tests and the worst outcomes in terms of employment and further education. The most striking feature of the generally low levels of familial integration and involvement of the young with adults in West Indian households was a 41 per cent level of paternal absenteeism and only a 37 per cent marriage rate, together with the highest rates of overall conflict and poor level of play and other materials at home. That the comparative paucity of the domestic environment and family relationships may have lain behind poor performance received support from the observed differences between Asian groups. The ones that did least well came from homes with the most conflict, largest numbers of children, lowest provision for adult-child activities and poorer parent/child relations.[69]

Paternal involvement with children is associated with facilities upon which mutual pursuits, and thus developmentally beneficial and mutually enjoyable activities, are based. These, and factors like home maintenance, all have a greater tendency to decline with paternal detachment or absenteeism. It is probably a combination of an ethos which maintains a high degree of parental involvement and home centredness, extended kin support, and the preservation of the deceased husband's memory as a positive role model, which accounts for the more favourable outcomes for children of widows compared with those from backgrounds of divorce or unwed motherhood.

Using their longitudinal study of 700 Nottingham children, the Newsons and Charlie Lewis found that father participation in middle childhood encouraged educational achievement and career plans, as well as preventing later lawlessness, as measured by criminal records, and surpassed any relationship with disciplinary styles or temperament.[70] Similarly, when the children from the National Child Development Study were sampled in the mid-1970s, it was found that a child's attainment in school was so closely related to the father's interest in the child's progress that even such small matters as his willingness to go with the mother and discuss the child with the teacher had large measurable results on achievement in basic subjects.[71]

Deconstructing Father
Those who wish to maintain, in the face of mounting evidence to the contrary, that the disadvantages experienced by children

from broken or lone-parent family backgrounds can be explained in terms of economic variables have been forced to widen the use of the term 'economic'. Virtually every aspect of a child's upbringing can become just another 'economic' variable.

The major case in point is the interpretation of evidence from the British National Child Development Study, which began with the 17,414 children born in March 1958 who, in declining numbers, have been sampled at 7, 11, 16, 23, and 33, with far higher drop-out rates for those with lone parents or stepfamilies. As already seen, E. Crellin and colleagues had found that children born illegitimate had lower scores on tests of attainment at 7 compared with the legitimate and, as in other studies, the gap was bigger at the non-manual class level. At 11 and 16, those who had experienced marital breakdown also had lower scores as well as poorer behaviour and adjustment. While some of the reading and maths differences had occurred before some homes broke up, divorce widened the gap. But researchers now explain how the 'relatively low test scores overall' of children who had lived with a lone parent at any time might be seen as reflections of their poor material circumstances rather than the absence of one parent *per se*. In this usage 'material' includes not only financial but social circumstances.[72] So adjustment was simultaneously made for factors which included not only social class and income, but household tenure, mother's education and employment, the number of schools attended, amenities and maintenance at home, parental aspirations, whether home had a room for homework, the child's sex and whether the child had been in care—as a significant proportion of lone-parent children had been. Clearly, some outcomes of parental absenteeism (e.g. going into care) are being used as causes of others (e.g. lower school scores). Unsurprisingly, this re-interpretation of the data significantly reduced the differences in the mean test scores between those from one- and two-parent families. Children with both parents no longer had higher reading scores, although the differences for maths were only reduced by about half.

This might be seen as an example of paternal disaggregation, or the abstraction of each of the father's activities or contributions, and amounts to a re-definition of lone parenthood. It has been compared to the way in which "disaggregating Hurricane Andrew into wind, rain and tides can make it disappear as a meteorological phenomenon".[73] It then becomes their lack which affects outcomes, not the absence of the father to perform them. Accounts of the actual cases in which family excursions, house maintenance or keeping children out of care are not happening because a parent is missing, become difficult to distinguish from suggestions that the activity might be performed by someone else. Thus a substitute for paternal input might encompass everything from decorating services to compensatory education, or mothers could be economically and morally primed to be 'strong' women able to make up any shortfall.

If it is only 'processes' of child rearing which matter then, as Anna Coote, Harriet Harman and Patricia Hewitt seem to suggest, families can become as fluid as desired without adverse consequences for the children. Thus, what "counts is not whether parents are divorced or he has been raised in a one-parent family", but "the quality of his relationships ... with his natural parents and with other parent figures with whom he forms a close bond", and this is "especially important when the marriage breaks down and the father leaves the home".[74] They will be pleased to hear that, according to David Utting and colleagues in the quasi-official *Crime and the Family*, "The statistical connections [with delinquency], as has been seen, are either insignificant or the result of indirect influences over the way that children are socialised".[75] It is difficult to see on what the conclusion about 'insignificant connections' is based when, among studies which Utting and colleagues themselves list, is M.E.J. Wadsworth's work on the criminal records of the 1946 birth cohort of the National Survey of Health and Development. Here, boys who had been through marital breakdown were more likely to be in custody, and those who had been young at the time of the break were twice as likely to be delinquent by the age of 21 and to have been convicted of serious offences.[76] After controlling for adverse financial conditions attributable to disruption, the relationship between broken homes and subsequent delinquency still remained. Also noted is D.J. West's and D.P. Farrington's longitudinal study of London youths, with its high rates of parental separation among the 50 men who had been convicted as juveniles and adults.[77]

In spite of this, Utting and colleagues prefer to rely on a 1982 study by Joan McCord, which was based on a follow-up of men who had been part of a counselling programme for delinquency prevention as children between 1939 and 1945.[78] The data were from old treatment records, and no information was provided on the selection procedure or socio-economic background of the sample, except that it contained both "average" and "difficult" youngsters from congested areas of Massachussetts. About a third came from homes broken by the absence of the natural father, although there is no indication as to whether this was the result of widowhood or other causes. A substantial proportion of both present and absent fathers were, however, known criminals and alcoholics. It was found that men from unbroken homes with serious conflict were more criminal than those from either unbroken or broken homes with affectionate mothers. This unremarkable finding has been seized upon by those anxious to argue that family background makes no difference at all to criminal propensities.

However, it would be wrong to stop here and conclude that mothers' nurturing love is sufficient, as well as being equally available in different types of household. If we read on, we find that "supervision, a form of control more likely to occur when a child was raised by two parents, accounted for a reliable proportion of the variation in crime". Certainly, where men had had affectionate mothers, non-deviant fathers, and supervision in childhood, outcomes for broken and unbroken homes were the same. Loving mothers were more likely to supervise, but then so were two parents and, despite the emphasis on the quality of parenting irrespective of the numbers of parents, "comparisons indicate that boys were more likely to be supervised if they had intact homes and were less likely to be criminal if supervised. The data could be interpreted as suggesting an indirect crimino-genic effect from paternal absence".[79] Unaffectionate broken homes provided very low levels of supervision.

David R. Offord's study of all juveniles placed on probation by the juvenile court of Ottawa-Carlton in the mid-1970s found that intact families had a significantly better chance of keeping anti-social behaviour under control if there were no other parental disabilities like mental illness, criminality and welfare history. Thus, "growing up in a one-parent family exposes a boy to a sufficiently increased risk of becoming delinquent such that other parental variables ... do not operate under these circumstances to increase further the risk of delinquency".[80] Utting and colleagues do not refer to Offord's work, although it appeared in the same book as Joan McCord's study.

As Deborah A. Dawson points out, while we know full well that family structure on its own is not a predictor of child development, it is a proxy for those factors that directly affect children's well-being. These might be the characteristics of the relations that accompany marital dissolution or intermittent cohabitation (for example, decreased attention, affection and communication), as well as factors that reflect the task overload of single parents.[81]

It is more accurate to speak of *intervening variables* when explaining why family structure is linked to outcomes. Economic status or poverty is also structural, but its effects depend upon intervening variables—although those who condemn references to family structure are often the same people who resort to simplistic economic explanations. A lone parent may be less capable of providing supervision, and *if* poor supervision is linked to delinquency, then there is an unavoidable link between disrupted families and criminality. As Dornbusch and colleagues report, the presence of other adults, like grandparents, brings household control levels closer to those of the two-parent family so, by the same token, "the raising of adolescents is not a task that can easily be borne by the mother alone".[82] Indeed, as Sara McLanahan emphasises: "whatever their capacities for managing their children, a couple can gang up on a teenager; a single parent cannot".[83]

However, variables like affection and even supervision—unless it refers simply to chaperonage—are affected by attachments. Those who speak of 'processes' almost suggest that it hardly matters who provides these as long as they are supplied at the requisite level from some source or another, so that the making and breaking of significant relationships is irrelevant. However, Judith S. Wallerstein and Sandra Blakeslee observed how the "children of divorce... taught us very early that to be separated from their fathers was intolerable".[84] In turn, John Tripp and Monica Crockett found that it is family reorganisation, particularly involving the father's departure, which is the main adverse factor in the lives of children involved in marital break up. This, not financial hardship or marital conflict, led to poor health, educational and social effects where the more transitions children experienced, the poorer the outcomes.[85]

The way in which the continuance, let alone quality, of the child's relationships with his natural parents is affected by whether they are divorced or the child is raised by a lone parent can hardly be ignored. Separated fathers often have a low level of involvement with their children—only a third had frequent, regular contact in the Tripp and Crockett study—and visiting men are poorly placed to become "other parent figures" described by Coote, Harman and Hewitt, with whom the child "forms a close bond".[86] Without the marriage structure, men often seem unable to "maintain their perspective as fathers or to hold in view the needs of their children".[87] There is reason to treat marriage as significant in its own right. Like other institutions, it brings order and security to people's lives and provides reference points outside of individual consciousness which shape attitudes and give coherence and direction to behaviour.

Just as the resident stepfather may have reduced incentives to invest in non-genetic children compared to his own offspring, so the non-resident father may also be disinclined to spend on absent children, even if they are his, because he has neither direct control nor benefit when it comes to the resources involved. As economist John Ermisch explains,[88] within marriage, spending on children increases the satisfaction of both parents and decisions on expenditure are likely to be collective ones. After divorce, the absent parent finds it difficult, if not impossible, to monitor the custodial parent's spending on the children. The proportion of child support which is spent on the child depends completely on the mother and, in any event, is unlikely to entail the whole amount. This inclines the father to reduce support. Thus, for any given level of family resources, expenditure on children is likely to be lower for divorced couples, if for no other reason than that the satisfaction derived by the father is much less. At the same time, the mother's social and economic investment in the children may be falling, not just because she has less income, but because she is more likely to be centring her life elsewhere, concentrating on her own interests and relationships.

One of the most sophisticated analyses, which helps us understand many other findings, is Ross L. Matsueda's and Karen Heimer's work on race, family structure, and delinquency.[89] Here, variables like parental supervision, attachment to peers and attitudes to delinquency may be seen as aspects of social control and association, which depend upon family and social background, like broken homes, socio-economic status and neighbourhood. Living in a troubled neighbourhood or a broken home is likely to weaken parental supervision, and low supervision increases delinquent peer relations, pro-delinquent attitudes and, ultimately, delinquent behaviour. However, broken homes foster pro-delinquent attitudes in ways that cannot be explained entirely in terms of supervision, perhaps by affecting moral beliefs and attachments. Hence, troubled neighbourhoods and broken homes both dilute the ties to parents, reduce the strength of conventional beliefs and increase the number of delinquent friends, compared with situations in which youths have warm relationships in intact families.

Catching Them Early

Parental assistance programmes, parental support programmes and parental education programmes sound like nice, sensible ways to improve outcomes for children, while avoiding the delicate subject of family structure. However, experience with parent training programmes suggests that success is often limited. Parents have to understand the principles involved, to be motivated to use them and successful in applying them. All in all, this can make it difficult to change parental behaviour.

Much has been made of the potential of compensatory early education to reduce later delinquency and school failure for children from disadvantaged family backgrounds. References are continually made to the Perry Preschool Project in Ypsilanti, Michigan, as if its results are typical of all nursery schooling or even day care. This was one of 11 demonstration projects or experiments to foster the intellectual development of poor, black, low IQ children that formed part of the Consortium of Longitudinal Studies in the 1970s and *the only one to have made a marked impact on later social problems.*[90] The girls were less likely to become pregnant as teenagers and, by 19, 57 per cent of the experimental group had two or more offences compared to 75 per cent of controls (for charges of serious crime it was 24 per cent to 38 per cent). As with the other Consortium projects, Perry children had lower rates of school drop out, having to repeat grades, or going into special education, and higher rates for completing high school and training. However, while the Perry children attended an educational programme for *12 hours a week* between the ages of three and five, teachers also paid weekly home visits. This kind of programme may have worked by enhancing the skill, confidence, motivation and aspirations of parents, as well as cultivating a more positive attitude in children towards achievement.

It is claimed even the original Perry Preschool Project was money well spent since, for every $1 invested, it was estimated to have saved $7 in terms of expenditure on special education, the criminal justice and penal system and lost tax revenue. But all the consortium projects operated with "ideal circumstances, skilled researchers, capable staff with lots of training, ample budgets". Those involved emphasised how, even if results like those of the Perry project could be repeated, it did not mean that they could ever be "reproduced in the kinds of projects that would characterise a program of national scope".[91] Since the projects were planned to maximise success, they might have been over lavish with resources, but it would be difficult to offer anything comparable with less than two qualified teachers trained in the Perry methods per 20 children, support programmes and systematic attempts to increase parental effort, particularly where all the input may have to come from one parent.

Unwarranted generalisation from model projects has been a factor in the way that the positive results of pre-school prog-rammes have been enormously exaggerated, and the assumption promoted that these will result from virtually any early non-parental care. With what has been called the 'Used Car Concept' in social programmes, an idea is oversold, the benefits exagger-ated, and the costs understated. Certainly, there have been short- and medium-term educational gains recorded for various British pre-school facilities, like well-run playgroups or nursery classes, but these are often small and sporadic and many studies show no positive long-term impact on intellectual or educational achievement. They count for very little compared to factors like parental education, parental involvement and parents' social and economic status.

The Social Network

As adolescence is the time when juvenile activity becomes most difficult for adults to monitor and control, it also now seems to be frequently envisaged that much of the role of families could be handed to professional agencies. Otherwise, mothers alone might experience particular difficulties with children of this age.

Accompanying the support services for parents of turbulent teenagers, it is recommended there be drop in resource centres, young adult centres, youth mediation schemes, peer-led drug prevention, and:

> ... 'detached' youth workers to make contact with young people in the places where they naturally congregate and provide a bridge with the local agencies that can best meet their needs.[92]

These are suggested as complementary to the children's centres, holiday activity schemes and after school clubs for school children from 5 years-old onwards, and day care for the under-fives.

It is difficult to see how all of these services could compensate for a general thinning of the number of responsible adults in the community, since marital and family disruption reduce the linkages in the network of social control as well as social support. This control is dependent upon more than the individual child's family, which is partly why, for example, a study of urban residents in two American centres found that the percentage of lone-parent households with teenagers was significantly associated with rates of burglary and violent crime.[93] The increase in one-adult households generally means that people in these atomised conditions are deprived of protection and control. This makes the number of unattached people in the community predictive of crime levels. A study of British estates found that, if the neighbours of lone parents are more likely to be victimised than the neighbours of two-parent households then, in turn, lone-parent households are more likely to be targets for crime.[94] Similarly, research by Douglas Smith and Roger Jarjoura shows that the greater the percentage of lone parents with children in American neighbourhoods, the higher the rates of crime and burglary. Rates of family disruption are not the only factor. Population density, mobility and the number of adolescents matter as well. What, by itself, did *not* seem to matter was the number of low-income families in a neighbourhood.[95] In turn, data from the National Longitudinal Survey of Youth found that, while young black men with lone mothers were twice as likely to engage in criminal activities compared with those raised by two parents, after holding constant variables like income, parental education and residence, growing up in a neighbourhood with high rates of family fragmentation tripled the possibility.[96]

It is easier for two-parent families to act when it comes to general youth neighbourhood surveillance, intervention in disturbances and control of peer group activities, like 'hanging around', vandalism and truancy, that often become the overture for more serious crime and gang delinquency. Areas with high rates of family disruption tend to have low rates of participation in community politics, recreation and educational activities as lone mothers participate less than married women in social and educational organisations. The same is true for single men compared to fathers. Communities with pronounced family disruption may experience a weakening of formal and voluntary organisations, many of which play crucial roles in linking youth to wider social institutions and fostering desired principles and values.[97] The social disengagement that follows from family fragmentation militates against the proposals for residents to manage schools, set up youth activities, serve as volunteers and on management committees, and even regenerate local economies, which are recommended to secure more cohesive neighbourhoods.

Marriages:

> ... are the rivets of the social order, local level attachments by which the whole structure is ultimately assembled.[98]

When a couple marry, they initiate a whole series of exchanges involving two groups of people, or the relatives and friends on each side. Over time, as the developmental cycle of the family continues in motion, the web of kinship makes up the strongest threads in the structure of community. Kinsmen, as 'the formal actors of the moral order, bound to us by sanctions, duties and rights', are not just a personal social security system, with people to help when things go wrong or set an example, they also create affiliative and integrative patterns.

The social structure implied by policies supporting the lone mother as the basic or pre-eminent 'family form' is what Gerald Suttles,[99] in his work on the slum, refers to as ordered segmentation. Here separate sex, age, territorial and ethnic units operate without webs of interlinked relationships, with segregation, as much as disintegration, built into the social system. With few individual ties, society resembles a series of building blocks, with proximity but little interaction between the members, instead of a network of overlapping and mutually supportive interdependencies.

A Warrior Class?

The impact of lone parenthood on the absent men is probably the least considered consequence of the rise of lone parenthood. Yet it is of immense and fundamental significance for public order and economic productivity. The family man role as much provides men with incentives for orderly and patient participation in the community as it is a source of discipline for children. As Geoff Dench has observed from his investigation of changing West Indian family structure, when men abandon responsibility for their children "many are effectively abdicating from any responsibility in the community. A man who does not recognise claims of dependants on him loses those external demands on himself which could raise him above his own immediate or short-term desires".[100] Thus, instead of neighbourhood standards being enforced by fathers, low marriage rates mean a decline of the responsible male and an increasing likelihood that men are going to be net contributors to the community's problems.

> Single men are troublesome, and difficult for the community to control. Marriage is an extremely valuable instrument for tying them down and channelling their energies into socially useful ends. ... to achieve this end, conventions about husbanding and fathering typically exaggerate the real importance of the contributions which men make to family life, so that men are flattered into feeling that they are really needed.[101]

Support for mothers independently of men is not only the effect of hostility to men as providers, in particular, and derogation of their contribution to families, in general, but seems to make it self-evident that men are dispensable for childrearing. What Alan Tapper reports for Australia can also be said of the image of the irrelevant father that the lone-parent campaign puts over in Britain:

> ... as a result of welfare policy, Aboriginal families are tending to become matricentric and to 'socially repress the significance of fathers altogether'. He [Jeff Collman, anthropologist] concludes that 'because women have privileged access to welfare resources, they often have more secure domestic livelihoods than men, and men often depend upon them for their more basic requirements'. The conditions under which women acquire welfare benefits, however, encourage them to minimise their relationships with men.[102]

The cost to the state of large numbers of unsupported mothers goes beyond the immediately identifiable welfare payments. Divorced men are up to eight times more likely to enter psychiatric hospitals, and single men nearly three times more likely, than their married counterparts. Divorced individuals of both sexes make five-fold use of outpatient psychiatric services compared to the married, and over one in five divorced and separated men fall into the heaviest drinking category, compared to only 7 per cent of married men.[103]

The single male is far more likely to kill himself, and to be also disproportionately represented among the criminal and riotous.[104] While the effect of family disruption on crime is strongest for juveniles, family fragmentation is significantly related to adult criminality as well; indicative as it is of much instability, disorientation and conflict in adult relations.[105] Robert Sampson was able to show how a city's divorce rate was a better predictor of the robbery rate than were measures of arrest and sentencing.[106]

The same *anomie* and dislocation is present in the strong relationships between the suicides of young men and the out-of-wedlock birthrate and the number of persons living alone.[107] The suicide rates of both adults and children are also highly correlated with the divorce rate. This relationship holds even for the advanced Scandinavian welfare states, indicating that public services may be able to make little impression on the rise in young suicides in Britain, if family structure becomes increasingly unstable at the same time.[108]

Without marriage, society is deprived of the most successful corrective institution ever devised, as so many criminological investigations of recidivism will testify. Marriage also traditionally provided much of the explanation of why so many juvenile delinquents, even in the roughest areas, did so often grow out of misbehaving or 'drift out of delinquency'. David Matza has described how, as the gang boy grows up, his masculinity anxiety is "somewhat reduced when someone becomes a man rather than a mere aspirant". This is because, in the past, anyway: "Boys are less driven to prove manhood unconventionally through ... misdeeds when, with the passing of time, they may effortlessly exhibit the conventional signposts of manhood—physical appearance, the completion of school, job, marriage, and perhaps even children".[109]

People behave differently when they know that their actions will affect the standing in the community of those to whom they are formally connected. As David Murray explains:

> The worst social characterisation the Navajo can offer of a thoughtless, deviant man is the charge that 'he acts as if he had no relatives'. This phrase tells us that being embedded in relationships, in a network of legitimated and recognised kinsmen, is a powerful reinforcement for moral action.
>
> A man with no relatives, the Navajo feel, is a man with no concern for the shame or dishonour that his behaviour might bring upon those he loves. He acts, therefore, without control or humanity.[110]

Some argue that, as the entry level jobs have left the cities, and the state supports the mother-child unit, we have reproduced the historic conditions for a warrior class: separation of economic activity from family maintenance; children reared apart from fathers; wealth subject to predation and male status determined by combat and sexual conquest, with young men dealing in guns and drugs.[111] This momentous implication of lone parenthood is, as Geoff Dench alleges, studiously avoided by commentators in this country, where lone parents are discussed almost entirely in terms of how the mothers cope. There can be publications like *Crime and the Family* which completely ignore the impact of family breakdown on both adolescent control and the social involvement of men.[112]

Sometimes we find feminists brushing the issue aside with the insistence that men should not need families or employment prospects to behave themselves. Anyway, why should a woman want anything to do with men as destructive and futureless as many are now? If this strategy deprives the child of close contact with half the human race, it also excludes a half of the human race from the means to transcend immediate self-interest. Nobody learns and upholds social rules from outside social relations and responsibilities, but only by being in the midst of these and maintaining them because they are their own. People have to live and teach the lesson, if they are to know and abide by it themselves.

Compared with marriage, work probably provides a comparable focus for social integration for only a minority of men. Moreover, social integration through the family role is not just a barrier to troublesomeness, it is also the basis of much positive contribution. Its absence may weaken general processes of care and education in society, where one generation exerts itself on behalf of another. The psychoanalyst Erik Erikson spoke of generativity and investigation confirms how men, in this case adoptive fathers, are far more likely to adopt positions in organisations, formal and informal, that involve the guidance and welfare of younger people. Committed kinship thus builds other commitments. It is the foremost reservoir of altruistic social involvement, and shapes the moral capital of the next generation.[113]

Without this, the result is described by George Gilder as "the simultaneous emergence of a police state to suppress the men and of a child care state to manage the children".[114] This analysis is not limited to American conservatives, but shared with liberals like William Julius Wilson who, as in *The Truly Disadvantaged*, have drawn attention to the relations between family fragmentation and crime, violence and civil disorder, and their implications for policing and penal policy. The practical response to date has been to demand, build and plan for more prisons: six new ones are to be built in Britain over the next five years to hold 3,600 more inmates, plus five secure units for persistent young offenders between 12 and 14.

The more that women are helped to manage independently of men, and male self-esteem becomes detached from satisfactory performance as a family man, the more lower-class boys will drift through school failing to acquire skills. For middle-class men, the malaise may be post education, when there will be little incentive, apart from intrinsic interest, to make a concerted or consistent effort to advance in any concerted manner in any particular field. The fragility or absence of conjugal relations generally demotivates men, and all too easily promotes either a "child-like dependence in the family setting, or as welfare supported loners".[115] As they can opt out of almost all social obligations, men easily become dependants themselves and a "burden on their families, the community and society generally".

Unproductive Men

If supportive and compensatory resources for lone parents represent a major shift of personal services into the public domain so, at the same time, we must not only add the costs of more disturbed and disturbing lives, but the losses arising from the poorer work records of men uninvolved with families. Men freed from the need to worry about their relatives' welfare and living standards, have less incentive to work hard, especially in lower grade or unsatisfying jobs.

While the support a man can offer a family depends upon a number of factors, over which he may have little or no control, this does not alter the fact that marriage has a dramatic and positive impact upon male economic activity as much as on social responsibility. The rise in lone parenthood may be traced to the increasing numbers of men who have difficulties supporting families. As the labour market and taxation moved against them, they also found themselves in competition with the welfare system. Antagonism towards the family has speeded up the removal of its economic as much as its legal base, and the creation in Britain of the comprehensive system of support for the mother/child unit. But this leaves the men displaced from families without economic purpose. By reducing their motivation to better themselves, lone parenthood may limit male endeavours in education and employment. This may then have a general effect on wealth creation and productivity, as men disengage from economic activity.

The most significant aspect of the work of American authors of the new right will probably prove to be the way that they have drawn attention to those economic consequences of the feminisation of poverty which extend well beyond the plight of lone mothers, given that there is "no stronger nor more stable economic impulse than the drive to provide for one's family".[116] They are part of a long tradition of scholarship which relates marriage to a whole complex of behaviour basic to economic development. Malthus declared how this had to be presented to a youth as "a state peculiarly suited to the nature of man, and calculated greatly to advance his happiness". A strong conviction of its great desirableness must accompany the requirement that "the power of supporting a family was the only condition which would enable him really to enjoy its blessings".[117] These "powerfully urge him to save that superfluity of income which single labourers necessarily possess for the accomplishment of a rational and desirable object" instead of "dissipating it ... in idleness and vice".

As George Gilder developed the theme in his *Wealth and Poverty*, familial anarchy means that short-term male sexual rhythms prevail, and "boys are brought up without authoritative fathers ... to instil in them the values of responsible paternity: the discipline and love of children and the dependable performance of the provider role".[118] Poor communities are marked by the way that capital, in its human form of work effort combined with education and saving, does not adequately accumulate to provide income and wealth. If men's ties to the future through children are insufficient to induce work and thrift, the lack of family structure militates against extended production. It was through firm links between work, wealth, sex and children, that male energies were traditionally:

> ... directly tied to economic growth, and since strong sanctions were imposed on premarital sex, population growth was directly tied to economic productivity.[119]

There has been a long-standing undercurrent of male protest at marriage as financially burdensome and sexually repressive. This antedates modern feminism. The breadwinning role is seen as an onerous, emasculating burden and the 'good provider' as the dupe and drudge of women and children. They are the 'ball and chain' which keep his nose to the production line and away from more virile pursuits. This view is reflected in films, books, magazines, sports and elsewhere, which emphasise excitement, rejection of the prosaic discipline of work, a flair for conspicuous consumption, aggressive toughness as a proof of masculinity, and short-run hedonism. The authentic role of marriage in the control of men stands in sharp contrast to the view of marriage as the enslaver of women. Even Germaine Greer agrees that fatherhood imposes quite radical restrictions on men, who have to deny themselves the "anti-social satisfaction of seeing how many children they can sire, and cultivate instead a desire to be actively involved in the few they may sire".[120]

Traditionally, in working-class communities, marriage carried with it the right to be treated as adult and independent, and to be seen as socially adequate. Young husbands "felt they were now no longer simply youths out for a good time, but mature and responsible citizens".[121] This marked a welcomed rite of passage and demarcation from 'rough' elements for the young working-class male.

The disparity in the overall earnings of married and unmarried men (and women) reflects both the amount of time spent at work and effort. American analyses using 'earnings capacity utilisation rates', estimating how various groups make use of their labour market opportunities (controlled for age, credentials, opportunities, disability, and presumed discrimination) have shown married men working just about twice as hard as comparable single men, with effort often increasing with the number of children.[122]

In turn, levels of unemployment among widowed, divorced and separated men aged 16-64 were about twice the level of married men in Britain in the 1980s. Men in the National Child Development Study of 33-year-olds in 1991 were six times more likely to be economically inactive and over twice as likely to be unemployed if they were separated, divorced or widowed compared to the married, while single men were three times more likely to be unemployed or economically inactive and to derive all their income from state benefits.[123] Fathers are also substantially more likely to be in the labour force than men without dependent children (96 per cent to 63 per cent for the USA in 1987). Among husbands aged 45 years of age or older, 91 per cent of those with dependent children were in the labour force, compared to 54 per cent of those without.[124] In the short run, male employment is associated with marriage and higher fertility. Then the costs of raising children increase the economic demands on men. Over time, a fall in marriage or family size may contribute to a decline in labour force participation. Already, about 15 per cent of the fall in American male employment from 1960 to 1987 is directly attributable to the lower numbers with dependent children.

Research with couples underlines how marriage strongly affects a man's approach to work. He now has something to work for, and must keep going:

> The pressures that men were under were not only that they should keep in work, but also that they should do well at their job. Whenever an opportunity arose for advancement, greater responsibility or earning more money, these would be grasped; marriage seemed to provide a focus for striving.[125]

While the feminist view is that men 'use' their families for personal gain, husbands chiefly see work as the means to improve the conditions and experience of family life, and concentrate on securing a standard of domestic living rather than occupational progress *per se*. Marriage is the "opportunity to establish a new identity as a *bona fide* adult", and:

> ... this new autonomy is inextricably linked with responsibility; indeed, marriage confers autonomy on the individual *because* it also confers responsibility. The act of getting married is, therefore, both liberating and restrictive. A job is no longer merely an activity which provides an income; it has become the means of sustaining a household and of carrying out those responsibilities which define adulthood.[126]

Little or no thought seems to have been given to what happens when the 'ideology of the male provider' disappears, with the systematic removal of men's capacity to support families, or how the education system is going to motivate boys "where they are not energised by a recognition of impending 'breadwinner' responsibilities".[127] If families without men need far more help and transfers than those with men, then men without families are far more likely to need assistance themselves.

There is, of course, the claim that women's job success will not only enable them to pay back the costs of child care and wage subsidies, but that they will make up for the shortfall in tax revenues and keep afloat the ship of public expenditure, weighed down by an under-motivated underclass of men. Not only can all lone mothers, indeed, all mothers, become entirely 'self-sufficient', but they will generate surplus revenue. Once the childcare arrives to deliver them of home responsibilities, there will even be a "productivity miracle in women's service sector work, so that this may be one of the great wealth generating engines of the future".[128] This is based on the notion of the post-industrial dawn, in which manufacturing industry will no longer matter to the prosperity of rich countries, whose economies will be devoted almost exclusively to services. Rich countries will buy the manufactured goods they need from poorer, industrialising countries. In return, the rich countries will offer sophisticated services, such as banking and consultancy.

The trouble is that there is no evidence that services are replacing manufactures in the exports of advanced countries. The share of services in the total exports of advanced countries has remained much the same for 25 years and has actually fallen for Britain since it lost its shipping fleets. Exports of financial services and such like have increased, but these are hardly to be equated with the catering or childcare or cleaning likely to absorb low-grade female labour, or provide employment for the poorly qualified lone parent who predominates in the welfare statistics. Indeed, as mothers generally have gone onto the labour market and taken work that they can shape around their family responsibilities, much of this represents the entry into the money economy of domestic production and is no addition to wealth. The major shift in the world division of labour is not from manufacturing to services, but a shift within the manufacturing sector itself. Here developing countries specialise in types of manufacture which use their abundant supplies of cheap, adaptable labour, while advanced countries specialise in areas where they might have a comparative advantage because of superior capital stock and skills. But then this shift to skill intensive work that puts the quality of a nation's labour force at a premium is unlikely to be advanced by demographic reproduction of low human capital, low labour market propensities, low income earning capacities, and dependency on public institutions.[129]

6

Conclusion

Into the Unknown

WE SEEM to be on the verge of an unprecedented social experiment,[1] considering that there has been no known human society built upon the mother/child unit. Indeed, for an anthropologist, a widespread failure to marry is a sign of impending disaster. All societies that have survived have been built on marriage, and children have always been raised within 'traditional' families. Even if some societies have had polygamy, and a few polyandry, while in others a number of married couples have lived in one household, it is still a truism that:

> Not only has there never been an open, democratic society not based on the family, there has never been any society of any sort not based on the family.[2]

For modern feminists, lone parenthood is often both a once and future state. In feminist demonology, male rights and responsibilities in relation to children, and patrial ties across and through the generations, are the expropriation of the products of women's bodies with kinship, marriage and inheritance. Thus the family is, from this perspective, an historical, and therefore transient, phenomenon which originated in a male usurpation, and which both can and should be overturned. Lurking here is Friedrich Engels's notion of the early stage of human history as one of promiscuity and communal provision, where no man claimed a link with any particular child and no child knew its own father.[3] Hence state support for mothers, as they make up their 'diverse family forms', is the return to conditions of primeval bliss where men, with no interest or investment in any particular child, all nonetheless contribute to a common pot into which the mothers dip for their own children—even if it has never been possible to give these fancies anthropological house room.

Let us repeat the little litany: Father-mother-child. We know the wealth of human values that this litany alludes to. Could a

152

similar wealth be hidden in the dyadic formula of mother-child? We doubt it very much indeed, if only because the exclusion of half of adult humanity from the central symbol of human love cannot possibly enhance humanity—it so obviously diminishes it.[4]

Instead, the transformation of reproduction from biological processes into morally and legally based institutions of kinship and marriage, probably marks the point at which social organisation emerged in evolutionary history. Fatherhood, that 'creation of society', exemplifies the rule-making and rule-following without which no culture is possible; and the appearance of altruism as obligation is most clearly expressed where men are bound to play a responsible part in the upbringing of their children.[5] Lone parenthood expresses a social factionalisation, rather than solidarity, and fragmentation, rather than integration. As it is marriage which has always been used to build "society's infrastructure, its bridges of social connectedness", and create moral sentiments of commitment and formal responsibility, we may find that the human costs of the continued erosion of the family become "socially, politically, and morally unacceptable".[6]

Certainly, a society in which men are peripheral will pose daunting problems of cohesion and control as well as leaving more children with inadequate adult supervision, compromised security, fewer adult role models and less intergenerational relationships. To enable mothers to 'go it alone' the state is moving in to substitute itself as the provider of the missing parent's functions, and to make good the loss of social capital for the children. It must also take over the family's role in nurturing those personal values and skills which enable communities to function. Yet it assumes these roles in the face of research findings which seriously question whether the state can ever discharge such functions adequately, especially in a social climate in which the client group of broken and incomplete families is increasing rapidly.

Of course, the replacement of the family with the mother/child unit is not the only historically unprecedented development facing us. There is also a population top-heavy with old people, in which workers increasingly labour to support the unrelated elderly, rather than their own children. Whether this offers any consolation is debatable, considering that expenditures on pensioners and lone parents represent the fastest-growing areas of public spending.

The move into a far more problematic form of childrearing is not so much the product of informed and free choice as, to no small degree, the result of the imposition upon society of a model designed to promote minority political objectives. The argument that we can only be the handmaidens of history amounts to little more than that élites hostile to the family, like all those who wage war, feel invincible if they enlist the gods to their cause in engineering a self-fulfilling prophecy. In this, the anti-family standpoint has closed off discussion, and permitted only one acceptable viewpoint and only one set of policies. According to the 10th Report on International Social Attitudes:

> Only four per cent [of the British] would advise a young woman to cohabit without eventually marrying, and only 12 per cent believe that personal freedom is preferable to the companionship of marriage. These and other answers suggest firmly that family life still reigns supreme as the desirable state.[7]

But rather than accept and build upon these common understandings and hopes, we have had to endorse the authors' preference for "various family forms, whether it be 'no families' [single and childless people], childless couples, or 'new families' [lone parents]" and agree that it would be no bad thing if traditional family values decline in order to accommodate women's greater "individual autonomy".

That there may be fewer families tomorrow has become justification for writing them off today, and thus for not supporting families who stay together as well as ones which break up. In the majority of cases children are still with their original parents. Eclipsed by the focus of publicity on the lone parent, members of intact families have passed from view. But, in the here and now, these families contain people as real as lone mothers and raise children as real as any lone parent's, even if it is repeatedly implied that such families do not, or should no longer, exist. The 1994 volume of statistics from the Office of Population Censuses and Surveys was hailed in the press with the declaration that "The nuclear family is dead ... laid to rest by the latest census of the nation's lifestyle".[8]

Simply on the basis of equity, the state should treat married parents as well as it treats divorced and single parents. This requires the elimination of all payments and services to broken families that are not made to intact families, with one benefit standard for all children, whether inside or outside the means-tested system, and personal and dependent tax exemptions. This will enhance family security and reduce welfare dependency. Men who stay with families should not be penalised as at present. Since the decline in intact families cannot be separated from the labour market tribulations of men, there is the need for employment opportunities for men, that are as considerate and 'friendly' to family providers, as they are now often asked to be towards parents as carers. In such ways, we signal that family stability is very important for children and for society as a whole, that both parents matter and that the way in which they wish to meet the childrearing task deserves recognition and respect.

Table 1.1

People in Households:
by Type of Household and Family in which They Live

Great Britain	Percentages				
	1961	1971	1981	1991	1992
Living alone	3.9	6.3	8.0	10.7	11.1
Married couple, no children	17.8	19.3	19.5	23.0	23.4
Married couple with dependent children	52.2	51.7	47.4	41.1	39.9
Married couple with non-dependent children only	11.6	10.0	10.3	10.8	10.9
Lone parent with dependent children	2.5	3.5	5.8	10.0	10.1
Other households	12.0	9.2	9.0	4.3	4.6

Source: *Social Trends 24*, Central Statistical Office.

Table 1.2

Marriage and Divorce Rates, England and Wales, 1971-1991

Year	All marriages	First marriages		Remarriages		Divorces
	Persons marrying per 1,000 of all ages	No. marrying per 1,000 single aged 16 and over		No. remarrying per 1,000 widowed or divorced		Persons divorcing per 1,000 married
		Bachelors	Spinsters	Men	Women	
1971	16.5	82.3	97.0	70.4	18.5	5.9
1976	14.5	62.8	76.9	79.3	24.1	10.1
1981	14.2	51.7	64.0	71.0	23.5	11.9
1986	13.9	44.6	55.7	58.9	22.2	12.9
1991	12.0	37.0	46.9	44.0	18.6	13.5

Source: *Marriage and Divorce Statistics*, Series FM2, OPCS

Table 1.3

Distribution of the Different Types of Families with Dependent Children, Great Britain, 1971-1991

Type of family with dependent children*	Percentage of all families with dependent children				
	1971	1981	1986	1990	1991 (Prov)
One-parent families					
Single lone mothers	1.2	2.3	3.2	5.9	6.4
Separated lone mothers	2.5	2.3	2.6	3.5	3.6
Divorced lone mothers	1.9	4.4	5.6	6.2	6.3
Widowed lone mothers	1.9	1.7	1.1	1.1	1.2
Lone mothers	7.5	10.7	12.5	16.8	17.5
Lone fathers	1.1	1.4	1.4	1.6	1.4
Lone parents	8.6	12.1	13.9	18.4	19.0
Married couples** with dependent children	91.4	87.9	86.1	81.6	81.0
All families with dependent children	100 .0	100.0	100.0	100.0	100.0

Source: *Population Trends 71*, drawn from General Household Survey.

* Dependent children are defined as aged under 16, or from 16 to 18 and in full-time education, and living in the family.

** Includes some cohabiting couples.

Table 1.4

Dependent Children in One-Parent and Married Couple Families,
1981-1991, Great Britain

Type of family with dependent children*	Average number of dependent* children per family				
	1981	1986	1988	1990	1991 (Prov)
One-parent families					
Single lone mothers	1.2	1.3	1.4	1.4	1.5
Separated lone mothers	1.8	1.8	1.9	2.0	2.0
Divorced lone mothers	1.8	1.8	1.7	1.8	1.9
Widowed lone mothers	1.4	1.4	1.5	1.6	1.6
Lone mothers	1.6	1.6	1.6	1.7	1.7
Lone fathers	1.6	1.4	1.5	1.5	1.6
Lone Parents	1.6	1.6	1.6	1.7	1.7
Married couples** with dependent children	2.1	1.8	1.8	1.9	1.9
All families with dependent children	2.0	1.8	1.8	1.8	1.8

Source: *Population Trends 71*, drawn from General Household Survey

Note: all estimates are based on 3-year averages, apart from 1991 estimates (1971 estimates are based on 1971-73 data).

*   Dependent children are defined as aged under 16, or from 16 to 18 and in full-time education, and living in the family.

**   Includes some cohabiting couples.

Table 1.5

Individuals in the Bottom 10 Per Cent of the Income Distribution
(After Housing Costs), Analysed by Family Type

	1979	1988/89	1990/91
Percentage whose family type is:			
pensioner couple	20	6	6
single pensioner	11	8	5
couple with children	41	44	49
couple without children	9	10	12
single with children	9	10	11
single without children	10	22	18
All family types (%)	100	100	100

Source: Department of Social Security, *Households Below Average Income 1979-1990/91.*

FAREWELL TO THE FAMILY?

Table 5.1

Number of Children 5-17 Years of Age and Mean Overall Behavioural Problems Score Per Child, by Family Type and Selected Demographic and Social Characteristics: United States, 1988

Characteristics	All Children*	Biological mother and father	Formerly married mother and no father	Never-married mother and no father	Mother and step-father
Total**	45,144	25,945	5,712	2,702	5,132
Total**	6.19	5.42	7.34	8.16	7.10
Annual Family Income ($)					
Less than 10,000	7.91	6.15	8.69	8.55	8.34
10,000-19,999	7.21	6.65	7.59	8.23	8.82
20,000-34,999	6.06	5.44	6.71	7.45	7.14
35,000-49,999	5.75	5.35	5.84	12.07	6.95
50,000 or more	5.33	4.89	6.52	8.75	6.31

Source: US Department of Health and Human Services.

*   Including other and unknown family type.

**   Including children with other and unknown values on individual demographic and social characteristics.

Figure 1

Births Within Marriage and Outside Marriage as Components of Total Period Fertility Rates, 1978-1992

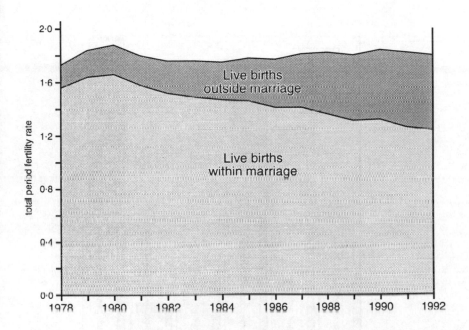

Source: Birth Statistics, Series FM1, OPCS.

Note: The total period fertility rate (TPFR) indicates the average number of children a woman will have over her lifetime. A TPFR of 2.1 is required for the population to replace itself.

Figure 2

Number of Persons in the UK With Incomes Below
Benefit Level but not Receiving Income Support
or Supplementary Benefit, by Family Type
1979 and 1989

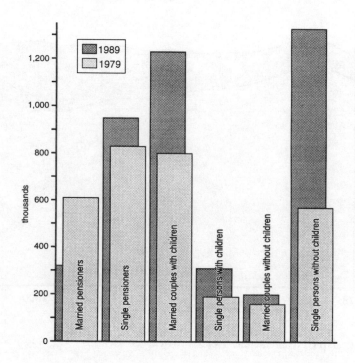

Source: Department of Social Security, Social Security Committee, *Low*
           Income Families 1979-1989.

Special Note: The number of pensioners in the population has increased rapidly, which means that although there has been a rise in the *number* of single pensioners falling below benefit level, as a *proportion* of all pensioners they have been falling. Entitlements for pensioners have risen over the period; if they had been held constant at 1979 levels, the number of pensioners falling below the benefit level would have fallen sharply in both the married and single categories.

Figure 3

*Individuals in the Bottom 10 per cent of the Income
Distribution (After Housing Costs)
by Family Type, 1990/91*

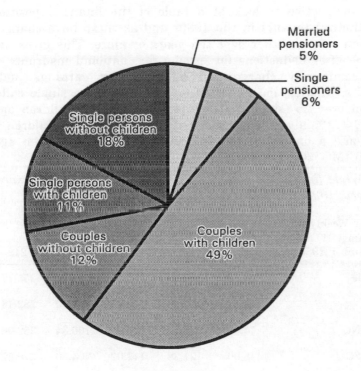

Married
pensioners
5%

Single
pensioners
6%

Single persons
without children
18%

Single persons
with children
11%

Couples
without children
12%

Couples
with children
49%

Source: Department of Social Security, *Households Below
Average Income 1979–1990/91.*

Appendix

Net Income after housing costs (equivalent value at April 1992) various household types, 1980-92

It is instructive to look at a table of the financial position of hypothetical tenants in the 1980s and as these have changed in relation to each other over ten years or more. This gives us net income after deductions for income tax, national insurance, rent and community charge and additions for earnings and all benefits, whether means-tested or universal, for a single childless person over 25 (single); a lone parent with two children aged 4 and 6 (LP); a one-wage married couple with no children (MC NC); and a one-wage married couple with two children aged 4 and 6 (MC 2C) at 1992 values.

NB: While figures for earnings are actual, net income is expressed in April 1992 equivalent values.

Gross Weekly Earnings (£) At November 1980	55	82	110	164	219
Single	60.69	85.20	118.26	182.03	253.77
LP	121.84	125.60	146.62	210.40	282.13
MC NC	77.38	96.49	126.55	190.34	262.06
MC 2C	118.09	121.28	141.02	204.80	276.52

Gross Weekly Earnings (£) At April 1983	74	111	147	221	295
Single	58.23	83.99	118.05	188.06	266.44
LP	117.03	123.57	145.77	215.78	294.16
MC NC	76.16	94.71	127.08	197.09	275.47
MC 2C	113.25	119.51	140.11	210.11	288.50

Gross Weekly Earnings (£) At July 1986	92	139	185	277	369
Single	60.32	96.26	135.32	213.43	301.89
LP	125.89	129.56	165.53	243.64	332.10
MC NC	83.71	106.35	145.40	223.51	311.97
MC 2C	122.00	123.26	159.23	237.34	325.80

Gross Weekly Earnings (£) at April 1989	120	180	240	360	479
Single	81.16	129.31	181.34	277.48	380.94
LP	128.24	156.46	208.85	304.62	413.08
MC NC	90.45	138.59	190.99	286.76	395.22
MC 2C	121.92	150.14	202.54	298.30	406.76

Gross Weekly Earnings (£) at April 1992	152	228	305	457	609
Single	91.81	141.97	192.79	297.79	398.74
LP	135.72	169.06	219.88	324.88	430.80
MC NC	95.09	144.96	195.78	300.78	406.70
MC 2C	125.51	157.94	208.76	313.76	419.68

The level of rents and community charge incorporated in the figures are based on national averages for the year 1992-93. With rents, this involves a considerable under-estimate of cost, because the rent figures for the third of council tenants whose housing costs are fully rebated are included in the calculation of the overall average figure. The figures also assume full take up of all benefits.

Source: Tax/Benefit Model Tables, Department of Social Security, published annually by the Government Statistical Service.

Notes

Chapter 1

1 Ermisch, J., *Fewer Babies, Longer Lives*, York: Joseph Rowntree Foundation, 1990; Haskey, J., "One Parent Families and Their Children in Great Britain; Numbers and Characteristics", *Population Trends 55,* 1989, pp. 27-33; Haskey, J., "Estimated Numbers and Demographic Characteristics of One-parent Families in Great Britain", *Population Trends 65*, 1991; Haskey, J., "Trends in the Numbers of One-parent Families in Great Britain", *Population Trends 71*, 1993, pp. 26-33.

2 For example, *Social Trends 24*, Central Statistical Office, 1994, p. 24.

3 Brown, A., "Family Circumstances of Young Children", *Population Trends 43*, OPCS, 1986, pp. 18-23.

4 Phoenix, A., *Young Mothers?*, Cambridge: Polity Press, 1990.

5 OPCS, *Birth Statistics 1992: England and Wales*, Series FM1, No. 21, p. xxiii, HMSO, 1994.

6 *Social Trends 24, op. cit.*, p. 34; and *General Household Survey 1992*, OPCS, HMSO, 1994.

7 Haskey, J., 1993, *op. cit.*, Burghes, L., *One Parent Families: Policy Options for the 1990s*, York: Joseph Rowntree Foundation, 1993. For married mothers with a child under five the employment rate doubled from 23 per cent to 45 per cent between 1981 and 1990, while for lone mothers the rate fell from 27 per cent to 22 per cent.

8 Millar, J., *Poverty and the Lone Parent*, Avebury, 1989.

9 *Hansard*, written answer, 26 February 1990, clms. 59-60.

10 Ferri, E. (ed.), *op. cit.*, 1993.

11 Seltzer, J.A., "Relationships between fathers and children who live apart: the Father's Role after Separation", *Journal of Marriage and the Family*, Vol. 53, 1991, pp. 79-101.

12 Bingley, P., Symons, E., Walker, I., "Child Support, Income Support and Lone Mothers", *Fiscal Studies*, Vol. 15, No. 1, 1994, pp. 81-98; also "The Effects of the 1986 Social Security Act on Family Incomes", *Findings,* Social Policy Research 54, York: Joseph Rowntree Foundation, 1994.

13 Roll, J., *Lone Parent Families in the European Community: The 1992 Report to the European Commission*, European Family and Social Policy Unit, 1992, p. 36.

14 *Evidence to Review of Benefits for Children and Young Persons*, National Children's Bureau, 1984, pp. 14-16.

15 Brown, J.C., *In Search of a Policy*, National Council for One Parent Families, undated, p.157; see also *Supporting Our Children: a briefing paper on the government's proposals on maintenance for children*, Family Policies Studies Centre, 1991; and Bradshaw, J. and Millar, J., *Lone Parent Families in the U.K.*, HMSO, 1991.

16 Social Security Committee 1992, *Low Income Families 1979-89*, Second Report, 1992-3 Session.

17 Giles, C. and Webb, S., *Poverty Statistics: A Guide for the Perplexed*, Institute of Fiscal Studies, 1993; *Households Below Average Income 1979-1990/91*, Department of Social Security, 1993.

18 Rowlingson, K., and Kempson, E., *Gas Debt and Disconnections*, Policy Studies Centre, 1993, p. 92.

19 Bradshaw, J., *Household Budgets and Living Standards*, York: Joseph Rowntree Foundation, 1993.

20 Millar, J., *Poverty and the Lone Parent*, London: Avebury, 1989; also Bradshaw, J. and Millar, J., *Lone Parent Families in the UK*, London: HMSO, 1991.

21 *Key Facts*, November 1993, National Council for One Parent Families referring to Institute of Housing Survey, October 1993; also *Lone Parents and Housing*, Research Paper 94/11, 18 January 1994, House of Commons Library.

22 See, Haskey, J., "Trends in the Numbers of One-Parent Families in Great Britain", *op. cit.*

23 Kempson, E., Bryson, A. and Rowlingson, K., *Hard Times?*, London: Policy Studies Institute, 1994.

24 Rowlingson, K. and Kempson, E., *op. cit,* p. 23.

25 *The Reform of Personal Taxation*, Cmnd. 9756, London: HMSO, 1986.

26 Marsh, A. and McKay, S., *Families, Work, and Benefits*, London: Policy Studies Institute, 1993; also *Lone Parents and Work*, Department of Social Security, Research Report No. 25, 1994.

27 Purves, L., "Let's Hear It From the Underclass!", *The Times*, 1 September 1993; and leader, *The Times,* 10 December 1992.

28 Giles, C. and Johnson, P., *Taxes Up, Taxes Down: The Effects of a Decade of Tax Changes*, London: Institute for Fiscal Studies, 1994; *Burden of Taxation*, Research Paper 94/66, House of Commons, March 1993; Kaletsky, A. and Bush, J., "Only the Very Rich Pay Less Income Tax Under the Tories", *The Times*, 13 January 1994; "The Effects of Taxes and Benefits on Household Income", *Economic Trends*, No. 483, January 1994.

29 Monk, S. (ed.), *From the Margins to the Mainstream,* London: National Council for One Parent Families, 1993, pp. 38-9.

30 Tapper, A., *The Family in the Welfare State*, Allen & Unwin and the Australian Institute for Public Policy, 1990, pp. 194-95.

31 *The Report of the Committee on One Parent Families* (The Finer Report), Vol. 1, London: HMSO, 1974.

32 Brown, J.C., *op. cit.,* p. 129.

33 Graham, H., "Women's Poverty and Caring", in Glendinning, C. and Millar, J. (eds.), *Women and Poverty in Britain*, Wheatsheaf, 1987, p. 226.

34 *The Report of the Committee on One Parent Families* (The Finer Report), Vol. 1, London: HMSO, 1974.

35 *The Reform of Social Security,* Vol. 2, London: HMSO, 1985, p. 48.

36 Brown, J.C., *op. cit.,* p. 157.

37 As, for example, Bush, J., "Helping with Childcare Can Cut the Cost of Lone Parents", *The Times*, 2 September 1993.

38 Holterman, S., *Becoming a Breadwinner*, The Daycare Trust, 1993.

39 Heclo, H., "The Political Foundations of Anti-Poverty Policy", in Danziger, S.H. and Weinberg, D. H., *Fighting Poverty: What Works and What does not*, Harvard University Press, 1986; and Preston, S.H., "Children and the Elderly: Divergent Paths for America's Dependants", *Demography*, Vol. 21, No. 4, 1984, pp. 435-54.

40 Piven, F., "Women and the Welfare State: Ideology and the Welfare State", in Rossi, A.S. (ed.), *Gender and the Life Course*, New York: Aldine, 1985, p. 266.

41 Dench, G., *From Extended Family to State Dependency,* Centre for Community Studies, Middlesex University, 1993, p. 73.

42 Toynbee, P., "The Worm Turned Syndrome", *The Observer*, 10 September 1989.

Chapter 2

1 Davies, H., economist, Birkbeck College, quoted by Bush, J., "Helping with Childcare Can Cut the Cost of Lone Parents", *The Times*, 2 September 1993.

2 Giles, C. and Webb,S., *Poverty Statistics: A Guide for the Perplexed*, London: Institute for Fiscal Studies, 1993; and Roll, J., *Understanding Poverty*, Occasional Paper No. 15, London: Family Policy Studies Centre, 1992; and "Households Below Average Income 1979-1990/1", Department of Social Security, 1993.

3   *Hansard*, written answers 5 November 1993, Col. 589-90, and 8
    February 1994, Col. 219-20.

4   Murray, C., *Losing Ground: American Social Policy 1950-1980*,
    New York: Basic Books, 1984, p. 130.

5   See for American poverty income and demographic trends and
    statistics Ellwood, D.T., *Poor Support: Poverty and the American
    Family*, New York: Basic Books, 1988; Danziger, S.H., and
    Weinberg, D.H., (eds.), *Fighting Poverty: What Works and What
    Does Not*, Harvard University Press, 1986; Cottingham, P.H. and
    Ellwood, D.T., (eds.), *Welfare Policy for the 1990s*, Harvard
    University Press, 1989; Hewlitt, S.A., *When the Bough Breaks*,
    Basic Books, 1991; *Child Neglect in Rich Nations*, UNICEF,
    1993; and Jencks, C. and Peterson, P.E., *The Urban Underclass*,
    Washington DC: Brookings Institution, 1991.

6   Murray, C., *op. cit.*, p. 176.

7   Millar, J., *Poverty and the Lone Parent: the Challenge to Social
    Policy*, Avebury, 1989, p. 186; see also Millar, J., "Lone Mothers",
    in Glendinning, C. and Millar, J. (eds.), *Women and Poverty in
    Britain*, Wheatsheaf, 1987.

8   Burghes, L., *One Parent Families: Policy Options for the 1990s*,
    London: Family Policy Studies Centre, 1993, p. 42.

9   Joshi, H. "The Cost of Caring", in Glendinning and Millar, *op.
    cit.*, p. 131.

10 Ferri, E., *Life at 33*, National Childrens' Bureau, 1993.

11 Coote, A., Harman, H. and Hewitt, P., *The Family Way*, Institute
    of Public Policy Research, 1990, p. 36.

12 Glendinning, C. and Millar, J., *op. cit.*, p. 25.

13 Toynbee, P., "A Woman's Work is Never Done", *The Sunday
    Times Review*, 14 September 1991.

14 Ward, C., Joshi, H. and Dale, A., "Income Dependency Within
    Couples", National Child Development Study, Working Paper,
    No. 36, 1993, pp. 5-6.

15 Glendinning, C. and Millar, J., *op. cit.*, p. 24.

16 As in Coote, A., Harman, H. and Hewitt, P., *op. cit.*

17 There are now many accounts of household expenditure
    allocation, usually hostile to marriage and out to prove that
    women lose out whatever the arrangement. See Pahl, J., *Money
    and Marriage*, Macmillan, 1989; and Wilson, G., *Money in the
    Family*, Avebury, 1987.

18 Kempson, E., Bryson, A. and Rowlingson, K., *Hard Times?*,
    London: Policy Studies Institute, 1994.

19 Brannen, J. and Wilson, G., *Give and Take in Families*, Allen &
    Unwin, 1987, p. 16.

20 See Land, H., "Poverty and Gender: the Distribution of Resources within Families", in Brown, M. (ed.), *The Structure of Disadvantage*, Heinemann, 1983; and Graham, H., *Women, Health and the Family*, Wheatsheaf, 1984.

21 Glendinning, C. and Millar, J., *op. cit.*, p. 10; and see Payne, S., *Women, Health and Poverty*, Harvester, 1991, p. 38.

22 Glendinning and Millar, *op. cit.*, p. 6.

23 Lister, R., *Women's Economic Dependency and Social Security*, Equal Opportunities Commission, 1992, p. 20.

24 Glendinning and Millar, *op. cit.*, p. 24.

25 *Ibid.*, pp. 5-6.

26 Banks, J. and Johnson, P., *Children and Household Living Standards*, London: Institute for Fiscal Studies, 1993.

27 Moss, P., *Childcare and Equality of Opportunity: Consolidated Report to the European Commission*, April 1988, pp. 26-28.

28 Investigations of women's losses over the childbearing years are based on the earnings forgone in childrearing spread over life. They usually avoid dealing separately with the matter of pay once the woman rejoins the labour force in a consistent way which, as it turns out, may be little different from that of women who never left. See Beggs, J.J. and Chapman, B.J., *The Foregone Earnings from Childrearing in Australia*, Discussion Paper 190, Canberra: ANU Centre for Economic Policy Research, 1988.

29 See Cohen, B., *Caring for Children,* Report for the European Commission's Childcare Network, 1988, p. 15; Lister, R., *Women's Economic Dependency and Social Security,* Equal Opportunities Commission, 1992; Joshi, H., *The Cash Opportunity Cost of Childbearing in Britain*, CEPR Discussion Paper, No. 157, 1987; Joshi, H., "Sex and Motherhood as Handicaps in the Labour Market", in McClean, M. and Groves, D. (eds.), *Women's Issues in Social Policy*, London: Routledge, 1991; Davies, H. and Joshi, H., "Sex, Sharing and the Distribution of Income", Birkbeck Discussion Paper, 1992. For antidote see Bank, J. and Johnson, P., *Children and Household Living Standards,* London: Institute for Fiscal Studies, 1993.

30 Graham, H., "Women's Poverty and Caring", in Glendinning, C. and Millar, J., *op. cit.*, p. 223.

31 See Land, H., *Women and Economic Dependency*, Equal Opportunities Commission, 1986.

32 Ward, C., Joshi, H. and Dale, Angela, *op. cit.*, p. 3.

33 Barrett, M. and McIntosh, M., "The Family Wage: Some Problems for Socialists and Feminists", *Capital and Class*, 1989, Vol. II, p. 55.

34 Caputo, R.K., "Patterns of Work and Poverty: Exploratory
    Profiles of Working Poor Households", *Families in Society: The
    Journal of Contemporary Human Services*, October 1991, pp.
    451-59.

35 Ellwood, D.T., *Poor Support, op. cit.*; also Ellwood, D.T. and
    Summers, L.H., "Poverty in America: Is Welfare the Answer or
    the Problem?", in Danziger, S.H. and Weinberg, D.H. (eds.),
    1986, *op. cit.*

36 Giles, C. and Webb, S., 1993, *op. cit.*

37 *Ibid*; and see also Ross, C., Danziger, S. and Smolensky, E., "The
    Level and Trend of Poverty in the United States", *Demography*,
    No. 24, November 1987, pp. 587-600.

38 Duncan, G.J. and Rodgers, W.L., "Longitudinal Aspects of
    Childhood Poverty", *Journal of Marriage and the Family*, 50,
    1988, pp. 1,007-21; Danziger, S.H., Haveman, R.H. and Plotnick,
    R.D., "Antipoverty Policy: Effects on the Poor and the Nonpoor",
    and Bane, M.J., "Household Composition and Poverty" with
    Introduction by Danziger, S. and Weinberg, D. in Danziger, S.H.
    and Weinberg, D.H., 1986, *op. cit*; Besharov, D.J., "Targetting
    Long-term Recipients", in Cottingham, P.H. and Ellwood, D.T.,
    op. cit.

39 Ellwood, D.T. and Summers, L.H., "Poverty in America: Is
    Welfare the Answer or the Problem?", in Danziger, S.H. and
    Weinberg, D.H., *op. cit*, 1986; and Danziger, S.H. and
    Gottschalk, P., *Uneven Tides: Rising Inequality in America*, New
    York: Russell Sage Foundation, 1992; and Levy, F., *The
    Changing American Income Distribution*, New York: Russell
    Sage Foundation, 1987.

40 Danziger, S. "Fighting Poverty and Reducing Welfare
    Dependency", in Cottingham, P.H. and Ellwood, D., *op. cit.*, 1989.

41 Bradshaw, J., *Household Budgets and Living Standards*, York:
    Joseph Rowntree Foundation, September 1993.

42 Murray, C., *op. cit.*, p. 212.

43 Hewlett, S.A., *When the Bough Breaks,* Basic Books, 1991, p.
    141.

44 Millar, J., "Lone Mothers", in Glendinning, C. and Millar, J.
    (eds.), *Women and Poverty in Britain*, Harvester, 1987.

45 Duncan, G.J. and Rodgers, W.L., *op. cit.*

46 Ellwood, D.T., *Understanding Dependency: Choices, Confidence
    and Culture*, Washington DC: US Department of Health and
    Human Services, 1987.

47 Berstein, B., *Saving a Generation*, New York: Priority Press
    Publications, 1986, pp. 7-8, quoted in Novak, M. *et al.*, "The
    Working Seminar on Family and American Welfare Policy", *The*

New Consensus on Family and Welfare, American Enterprise Institute for Public Policy Research/Maquette University, 1987, p. 46.

48 Bane, M.J., "Household Composition and Poverty", in Danziger, S. and Weinberg, D., (eds.), *op. cit.,* 1986.

49 Lerman, R.I., "Child Support Policies", in Cottingham, P.H. and Ellwood, D.T., *op. cit.*, 1989, p. 233.

50 Walsh, A., "Illegitimacy, Child Abuse and Neglect and Cognitive Development", *Journal of Genetic Psychology*, Vol. 15, 1990. pp. 279-285.

51 Osborn, A.F., Butler, N.R. and Morris, A.C., *The Social Life of Britain's Five Year Olds*, Routledge & Kegan Paul, 1984.

52 Bernstam, M.S. and Swan, P.L., "Malthus and the Evolution of the Welfare State: An Essay on the Second Invisible Hand", Working Paper 89-012, Australian Graduate School of Management, University of New South Wales, 1989, pp. 3-4.

53 McLanahan, S., "Family Structure and the Reproduction of Poverty", *American Journal of Sociology,* 90, 1985, p. 873.

54 Freeman, R.B. and Holzer, H.J., "Young Blacks and Jobs–What We Now Know", *The Public Interest,* No. 78, Winter 1985, p. 27; Freeman, R.B., "Who Escapes", NBER Working Paper, 1986.

55 Craig, R., *The YTS: A Study of Non-Participants and Early Leavers*, MSC Research and Development No. 34, 1986; and Roll, J., *Young People at the Crossroads*, London: Family Policy Studies Centre, 1988; Main, B. and Shelly, M.E., "The Economic Effects of YTS", *Employment Gazette*, October, 1987; London: Department of Employment, Labour Force Surveys 1984 and 1991.

56 Gold, D. and Andres, D., "Development Comparisons between 10 year old Children with Employed and Non-Employed Mothers", *Child Development*, 49, 1978, pp. 75-84; also Bayder, N. and Brooks-Gunn, J., "Effects of Maternal Employment and Child Care Arrangements on Preschoolers' Cognitive and Behavioural Outcomes: Evidence from the Children of the National Longitudinal Survey of Youth", *Developmental Psychology*, Vol. 27, No. 6, 1991, pp. 932-45; Stafford, P., "Women's Work, Sibling Competition, and Children's Performance", *The American Economic Review*, 77, 1987, pp. 972-45.

57 Wedge, P. and Essen, J., *Children in Adversity*, Pan Books, 1982.

58 Aquilino, W.S., "Family Structure and Home-Leaving: A Further Specification of the Relationship", *Journal of Marriage and the Family*, 53, 1991, pp. 999-1,010.

59 Maclean, M. and Wadsworth, M.E.J., *The Interests of Children after Parental Divorce: A Long Term Perspective*, Centre for Socio-Legal Studies, Woolfson College, Oxford, Oxford University

Press, 1988; and abstract in *The International Journal of Law and the Family*, Vol. 2, 1988, pp. 155-66; Elliott, B.J. and Richards, M.P.M., "Children and Divorce: Educational Performance and Behaviour Before and After Parental Separation", *International Journal of Law and the Family*, 1991, pp. 258-276; Elliott, B.J. and Richards, M.P.M., "Parental Divorce and the Life Chances of Children", *Family Law*, November 1991.

60 Kuh, D. and Maclean, M., "Women's Childhood Experiences of Parental Separation and their Subsequent Health and Status in Adulthood", *Journal of Biosocial Science*, 22, pp. 121-35.

61 Crellin, E., Pringle, M.L.K. and West, P., *Born Illegitimate*, report for the National Children's Bureau, National Foundation for Educational Research, 1971.

62 Dawson, D.A., *Family Structure and Children's Health: United States 1988*, Series 10: 178 Vital and Health Statistics, Maryland: US Department of Health and Human Services, 1991.

63 Allison, P.D. and Furstenberg, F.F., "How Marital Dissolution Affects Children", *Developmental Pyschology*, 25, 1989, pp. 540-49.

64 Krein, F. and Beller, A.H., "Educational Attainment of Children from Single-Parent Families: Differences by Exposure, Gender and Race", *Demography*, Vol. 25, No. 2, 1988, pp. 221-335.

65 Wallerstein, J.S. and Blakeslee, S., *Second Chances*, New York: Ticknora Fields, 1989.

66 McLanahan, S., "The Consequences of Single Parenthood for Subsequent Generations", *Focus*, Institute for Research on Poverty, University of Winsconsin-Madison, 1988.

67 *Ibid,* p. 17; and McLanahan, S., "Family Structure and Dependency: Early Transitions to Female Household Headship", *Demography*, Vol. 25, No. 1, 1988, pp. 1-17.

68 Greenberg, D. and Wolfe, D.W., "The Economic Consequences of Experiencing Parental Marital Disruption", *Children and Youth Services Review*, 4, 1982, pp. 141-62.

69 Pilling, D., *Escape from Disadvantage,* The Falmer Press, 1990.

70 Lambert, L. and Hart, S., "Who Needs a Father?", *New Society*, Vol. 37, No. 718, 1976, p. 80.

71 McLanahan, S., "The Consequences of Single Parenthood for Subsequent Generations", *Focus*, Institute for Research on Poverty, University of Winsconsin-Madison, 1988.

72 McLananhan, S. and Bumpass, L., "Intergenerational Consequences of Family Disruption", *American Journal of Sociology*, Vol. 94, No. 1, 1988, pp. 130-152.

73 Keith, V.M., and Finlay, B., "The Impact of Parental Divorce on
    Children's Educational Attainment, Marital Timing, and
    Likelihood of Divorce", *Journal of Marriage and the Family*, Vol.
    50, 1988, pp. 797-809; and Kiernan, K.E., The Impact of Family
    Disruption in Childhood on Transitions Made in Young Adult
    Life", *Population Studies 46,* 1992, pp. 213-14; Miller, B.C. and
    Moore, K.A., "Adolescent Sexual Behaviour, Pregnancy and
    Parenting: Research Through the 1980s", *Journal of Marriage
    and the Family*, November 1991, p. 1,028.

74 Dornbusch, S.M. *et al.*, "Single Parents, Extended Households,
    and the Control of Adolescents", *Child Development*, 56, 1985,
    pp. 326-41; and Flewelling, R.L. and Bauman, K.E., "Family
    Structure as a Predictor of Initial Substance Use and Sexual
    Intercourse in Early Adolescence", *Journal of Marriage and the
    Family*, Vol. 52, 1990, pp. 171-81.

75 McLanahan, S., "The Consequences of Single Parenthood for
    Subsequent Generations", *Focus*, Institute for Research on
    Poverty, University of Winsconsin-Madison, 1988.

76 MacLean, M. and Wadsworth, M.E.J., *op. cit.*

Chapter 3

1   Murray. C., *Losing Ground: American Social Policy 1950-1980*,
    New York: Basic Books, 1984, p. 90.

2   *Ibid,* p. 163.

3   Itzin, C., *Splitting Up: Single Parent Liberation*, Virago, 1980,
    pp. 9-10; see also Bowskill, D., *Single Parents: A Compassionate
    Guide for the Divorced, the Separated and the Unmarried*,
    Futura, 1980.

4   Bennett, F., "The State, Welfare and Women's Dependence", in
    Segal, L., *What's to be Done About the Family?*, Penguin and the
    Socialist Society, 1980, p. 200; see also Bowles, S. and Gintis, H.,
    *Democracy and Capitalism: Property, Community and the
    Contribution of Modern Social Thought*, NY: Basic Books, 1988.

5   Moxnes, K., "Changes in Family Patterns—Changes in
    Parenting? A Change toward a More or Less Equal Sharing
    between Parents?", in Björnberg, U. (ed.), *European Parents in
    the 1990s*, Transaction Books, 1992, p. 225.

6   Levinger, G., "A Social Psychological Perspective on Marital
    Dissolution", in Levinger, G. and Moles, O.C. (eds.), *Divorce and
    Separation*, NY: Basic Books, 1979; Levinger, G., "Marital
    Cohesiveness and Dissolution: Integrative Review", *Journal of
    Marriage and the Family*, 27, 1965, pp. 19-28.

7   Becker, G.S., *A Treatise on the Family*, Harvard University Press, 1981.

8   Levinger, G., *op. cit.*

9   Ermisch, J., "Familia Oeconomica: A Survey of the Economics of the Family", *Scottish Journal of Political Economy*, Vol. 40, No. 4, 1993, pp. 353-75.

10 Dench, G., *From Extended Family to State Dependency*, Centre for Community Studies, Middlesex University, 1993, pp. 49-50.

11 Bernstam, M.S. and Swan P.L., "Malthus and the Evolution of the Welfare State: An Essay on the Second Invisible Hand", Working Paper 89-012, Australian Graduate School of Management, University of New South Wales, 1989.

12 Björnberg, U., "Parenting in Transition: An Introduction and Summary", in Björnberg, U. (ed.), *European Parents in the 1990s*, Transaction Books, 1992, p. 15.

13 Mansfield, P. and Collard, J., *The Beginning of the Rest of Your Life,* Macmillan, 1988; Lamb, M.E., Pleck, J.H. and Levine J.A., "Effects of Increased Paternal Involvement on Fathers and Mothers", in Lewis, C. and O'Brien, M., *Reassessing Fatherhood,* London: Sage, 1987.

14 Jordan, W., James, S., Kay, H. and Redley, M., *Trapped in Poverty*, Routledge, 1992.

15 Kempson, E., Bryson, A. and Rowlingson, K., *Hard Times?*, London: Policy Studies Institute, 1994.

16 McRae, S., *Young and Jobless*, London: Policy Studies Institute, 1987.

17 Cooney, T.M. and Hogan, D.P., "Marriage in an Institutionalised Life Course: First Marriage among American Men in the Twentieth Century", *Journal of Marriage and the Family*, 53, 1991, pp. 176-90.

18 Duncan, G.J. and Hoffman, S.D., "Teenage Underclass Behaviour and Subsequent Poverty: Have the Rules Changed?" in Jencks, C. and Peterson, P.E. (eds.), *The Urban Underclass*, Washington DC: The Brookings Institution, 1991.

19 Slack, P., *Poverty and Policy in Tudor and Stuart England*, Longmans, 1988.

20 Mare, R.D. and Winship, C., "Socioeconomic Change and the Decline of Marriage for Blacks and Whites", in Jencks, C. and Peterson, P.E., *op. cit.*

21 Wilson, W.J. and Neckerman, K., "Poverty and Family Structure: The Widening Gap between Evidence and Public Policy Issues", in Danziger, S.H. and Weinberg, D.H. (eds.), *Fighting Poverty: What Works and What Doesn't*, Harvard University Press, 1986.

22　Sampson, R.J., "Urban Black Violence: The Effect of Male Joblessness and Family Disruption", *American Journal of Sociology*, Vol. 93, No. 2, 1987, pp. 349-81; also Duster, T., "Crime, Youth Unemployment and the Black Urban Underclass", *Crime and Delinquency*, Vol. 33, No. 2, 1987; Mare, R. and Winship, C., "Socioeconomic Change and the Decline of Marriage for Blacks and Whites", in Jencks, C. and Peterson, P.E., *op.cit.*

23　Coward, J., "Conceptions Outside Marriage: Regional Differences", *Population Trends 49*, 1987; also Simms, M. and Smith, C., "Teenage Mothers and Their Partners: A Survey in England and Wales", DHSS Research Report No. 15, HMSO, 1986.

24　Kiernan, K.E. and Estaugh, V., *Cohabitation: Extra Marital Childbearing and Social Policy*, London: Family Policy Studies Centre, 1993.

25　McRae, S., *Cohabiting Mothers*, London: Policy Studies Institute, 1993, p. 105.

26　Tzeng, M., "The Effects of Socioeconomic Heterogamy and Changes on Marital Dissolution for First Marriages", *Journal of Marriage and the Family*, 54, 1992, pp. 609-19.

27　Lewis, S.N.C. and Cooper C.L., "Stress in Two Earner Couples and Stage in the Life Cycle", *Journal of Occupational Psychology*, 60, 1987, pp. 289-303; also Goldberg, W.A. and Easterbrooks, M.A., "Maternal Employment when Children are Toddlers and Kindergartners", in Gottfried, A.E. *et al.* (eds.), *Maternal Employment, Family Environment, and Children's Development: Infancy Through the School Years,* Plenum Press, 1988.

28　Ermisch, J., *Lone Parenthood*, Cambridge University Press, 1991.

29　Collard, J. and Thornes, B., *Who Divorces?*, Routledge and Kegan Paul, 1979.

30　Levinger, G., "Cohesiveness at the Brink: The Fate of Applications for Divorce", in Levinger, G. and Moles, O.C., *op. cit.*

31　See Fustenberg, Jr., F.F., "Premarital Pregnancy and Marital Stability", in Levinger, G. and Moles, O.C., *op. cit.*; and Kiernan, K.E., "Teenage Marriage and Marital Breakdown: A Longitudinal Study", *Population Studies*, Vol. 40, No. 1, 1986, pp. 35-54.

32　Haskey, J., "Social Class and Socio-Economic Differentials in Divorce in England and Wales", *Population Studies*, Vol. 38, No. 3, 1984, pp. 419-38; Lampard, R., "An Examination of the Relationship Between Marital Dissolution and Unemployment", Social Change and Economic Life Institute, Working Paper 17, 1990; Murphy, M.J., "Demographic and Socio-Economic Influence on Recent British Marital Breakdown Patterns", *Population Studies*, Vol. 39, No. 3, 1985.

33 Collard, J. and Thornes, B., *op. cit.*

34 Levinger, G., "Cohesiveness at the Brink: The Fate of Applications for Divorce", and Scanzoni, J., "Husband/Wife bargaining power and dissolution" in Levinger, G. and Moles, O.C., *op. cit.*

35 Rank, M.R., "The Formation and Dissolution of Marriages in the Welfare Population", *Journal of Marriage and the Family*, 49, 1987, pp. 15-20.

36 Jencks., C., "Is the American Underclass Growing?", Jencks and Peterson, *op. cit.*

37 Bertaux, D. and Delcroix, C., "Where Have All The Daddies Gone", in Björnberg, U. (ed.), *op. cit.*, pp. 186-7.

38 Moss, P. and Brannen, J., "Fathers and Employment" in Lewis, C. and O'Brien, M., *Reassessing Fatherhood*, London: Sage, p. 41.

39 Bassett, P., "More Men to do Women's Work as Part-time Trend Takes Hold", *The Times*, 16 February 1994.

40 *New Earnings Survey*, 1993.

41 Giles, C., and Webb, S., *Poverty Statistics: A Guide for the Perplexed*, Institute for Fiscal Studies; and Households Below Average Income Series, Department of Social Security. The figures for single, full-time workers include some lone-parents, but not more than a quarter, at most, of the total. It is the single *childless* workers who account for most of the growth in numbers.

42 Moynihan, D.P., *The Negro Family: The Case for National Action*, Washington DC: US Department of Labor, 1965; Wilson, W.J., *The Truly Disadvantaged*, University of Chicago Press, 1987.

43 Sampson, R.J., *op. cit.*

44 Bernstam, M.S. and Swan, P.L., "Brides of the State", *IPA Review*, 41, May-July 1987, pp. 22-79; Tapper, A., *The Family in the Welfare State*, Perth: Australian Institute for Public Policy, 1990; Bernstam, M.S. and Swan, P.L., "The State as Marriage Partner of Last Resort: A Labour Market Approach to Illegitimacy in the United States, 1960-1980", Kensington: Australian Graduate School of Management Working Paper 86-029, 1986.

45 Hill, M.A. and O'Neill, J., *Underclass Behavior in the United States: Measurement and Analysis of Determinants*, City University of New York: Baruch College, 1993.

46 *Lone Parents: Their Potential in the Workforce, NCOPF National Return to Work Programme: A Detailed Report*, National Council for One Parent Families, 1993.

47 Ellwood, D.T., *Understanding Dependency: Choices, Confidence or Culture?*, Division of Income Security Policy (ISP), US Department of Health and Human Services, 1987; Committee on Ways and Means of the US House of Representatives, *Background Material and Data on Programs within the Jurisdiction of the Committee on Ways and Means*, Washington DC: US Government Printing Office, 1989, pp. 536-37.

48 *Labour Force Survey*, London: HMSO, 1990, 1991.

49 Ashford, S., "Family Matters", in Jowell, R. *et al.* (eds.), *British Social Attitudes*, Gower, 1988; Scott, J., Braun. M. and Alwin D., "The Family Way", in Jowell, R. *et al.* (eds.), *International Social Attitudes: the 10th BSA Report*, SCPR, Dartmouth Publishing Co. Ltd., 1993.

50 *The 1992 Farley Report*, Farley Health Products Ltd., Nottingham.

51 McKay, S. and Marsh, A., *Lone Parents and Work: the Effects of Benefits and Maintenance*, Policy Studies Institute for the Department of Social Security, Research Report No. 25, 1994.

52 National Council for One Parent Families, *Lone Parents: Their Potential in the Workforce, op. cit.*

53 Bradshaw, J. and Millar J., *Lone Parents in the UK*, London: HMSO, 1991.

54 Martin, J. and Roberts, C., *Women and Employment: A Lifetime Perspective*, Department of Employment/OPCS, HMSO, 1991; Weale, A., *et al.*, *Lone Mothers, Paid Work and Social Security*, Bedford Square Press, 1984; Bradshaw, J. and Millar, J., *op. cit.*, 1991.

55 Roll, J., *Lone Parents in the European Community*, European Family and Social Policy Unit, 1992; Carlsen, S. and Larsen, J.E. (eds.), *The Equality Dilemma: Reconciling Working Life and Family Life, Viewed in an Equality Perspective*, Danish Equal States Council, 1993.

56 Ellwood, D.T., *Poor Support: Poverty and the American Family*, New York: Basic Books, 1988; Polit, D.F. and O'Hare, J.J., "Support Services", in Cottingham, P.T. and Ellwood, D.T. (eds.), *Welfare Policy for the 1990s*, Harvard University Press, 1989.

57 Parish, W.L., Hao, L. and Hogan, D.P., "Family Support Networks, Welfare, and Working among Young Mothers", *Journal of Marriage and the Family*, 53, 1991, pp. 203-15.

58 *Ibid.*, p. 209.

59 *Ibid.*, p. 214.

60 US Department of Labor, Employment and Training Administration, *The National JTPA Study: Title II-A Impacts on Earnings and Employment at 18 Months*, Research and Evaluation Report 93-C, Washington DC: US Department of Labor, 1993.

61 Zill, N., Moore, K., Ward, C. and Steif, T., *Welfare Mothers as Potential Employees: A Statistical Profile Based on National Data*, Washington DC: Child Trends Inc., 1991; Besharov, D.J., *US Welfare Reform*, paper prepared for the Institute of Economic Affairs by the American Enterprise Institute for Public Policy and Research, May 1994.

62 "Study finds that Education does not ease the Welfare Rolls", report on New Chance designed and evaluated by Manpower Demonstration Research Corporation, New York, *New York Times*, 22 May 1994,

63 Blum, M., *The Day-Care Dilemma*, Lexington, 1983; and Suransky, V.P., *The Erosion of Childhood*, University of Chicago Press, 1982.

64 Magnet, M., "Putting Children First: A New Direction for Welfare Reform", *City Journal*, New York: Manhattan Institute, Vol. 4, No. 3, 1994, pp. 47-52.

65 Plotnick, R.J., "Welfare and Out of Wedlock Childbearing: Evidence from the 1980s", *Journal of Marriage and the Family*, 52, 1990, pp. 735-46; Duncan, C.J. and Hoffman, S.D., "Teenage Behaviour and Subsequent Poverty", in Jencks, C., *op. cit.*

66 Kempson, E., *et al.*, *Hard Times?*, *op. cit;* Marsh, A. and McKay, S, *Families, Work and Benefits*, London: Policy Studies Institute, 1993; McLaughlin, E., *Flexibility in Work and Benefits*, Council on Social Justice, London: Institute for Public Policy Research, 1994.

67 Garfinkel, I. and McLanahan, S., *Single Mothers and Their Children: A New American Dilemma*, Washington DC: Urban Institute Press, 1986.

68 *Ibid.*

69 Winegarten, C.R., "AFDC and Illegitimacy Ratios", *Applied Economics*, Vol. 20, March 1988, pp. 1,589-1,601.

70 Plotnick, R.J., *op. cit.*

71 Ermisch, J., *Lone Parenthood*, Cambridge University Press, 1991.

72 Bernstam, M.S. and Swan, P.L., *op. cit.*, 1986.

73 Hardy, J.B. and Zabin, L.S., *Adolescent Pregnancy in an Urban Environment: Issues, Programs, and Evaluation*, Washington DC: The Urban Institute Press, 1991; Plotnick, R.D., "The Effect of Social Policies on Teenage Pregnancy and Childbearing",

Families in Society: the Journal of Contemporary Human Services, 1993, pp. 324-29.

74 Duncan, C.J. and Hoffman, S.D., "Teenage Behaviour and Subsequent Poverty", in Jencks, C. and Peterson, P.E., *op. cit.*

75 Ermisch, J., *op. cit.*

76 Researcher Kenneth Clarke, quoted in Wilson, W.J. and Neckerman, K.M., "Poverty and Family Structure", in Danziger, S.H. and Weinberg, D.H. (eds.), *Fighting Poverty: What Works and What Does Not*, Harvard University Press, 1986, p. 243; see also Ellwood, D.T. and Lerman, R., *Understanding Dependency: Choices, Confidence or Culture?*, Division of Income Security Policy (ISP), US Department of Health and Human Services, 1987; and Dash, L., *When Children Want Children: An Inside Look at the Crisis of Teenage Pregnancy*, Penguin Books, 1990.

77 Anderson, E., "Neighbourhood Effects on Teenage Pregnancy", in Jencks and Peterson, *op. cit.*, p. 389.

78 *Ibid.,* pp. 390 and 392.

79 Burgoyne, J., *Unemployment and Married Life*, Unemployment Unit Bulletin, 1985.

80 Becker, G., *op. cit.*, p. 80.

81 Department of Social Security, Tax/Benefit Model Tables, September 1992.

82 Jordon, W., *et al., op. cit.*

83 Ermisch, J., "Economic Influences on Birthrates", *National Economic Review,* November 1988; and *Fewer Babies, Longer Lives*, York: Joseph Rowntree Foundation, 1990.

84 Ferri, E. (ed.), *Life at 33*, National Children's Bureau and City University, 1993.

85 Bradshaw, J., *Household Budgets and Living Standards*, York: Joseph Rowntree Foundation, 1993.

86 *The Reform of Personal Taxation*, Cmnd. 9756, March 1986.

Chapter 4

1 Abramovitz, M., "Social Policy in Disarray: The Beleaguered American Family", *Families in Society: The Journal of Contemporary Human Services*, 1991, pp. 483-95; also Johnson, G.B., "American Families: Changes and Challenges", *Families in Society: The Journal of Contemporary Human Services*, 1991, pp. 502-10.

2 Carlson, A.C., "What happened to the family wage?", *The Public Interest,* Spring 1986, pp. 3-20.

3   Wilson, W.J. and Neckerman, K.M., "Poverty and Family Structure", in Danziger, S.H. and Weinberg, D.H. (eds.), *Fighting Poverty: What Works and What Does Not*, Harvard University Press, 1986; and Wilson, W.J., "Research and the Truly Disadvantaged", in Jencks, C. and Peterson, P.E. (eds.), *The Urban Underclass*, Washington DC: The Brookings Institution, 1991.

4   Dormor, D.J., *The Relationship Revolution*, London: One Plus One, 1992, p. 4.

5   Wicks, M., *The Daily Telegraph*, 11 October 1991.

6   Segal, L., "The Most Important Thing of All: Rethinking the Family", in Segal, L., *What's to be Done About the Family?*, Penguin and the Socialist Society, 1980, p. 18.

7   Björnberg , U., "Parenting in Transition: An Introduction and Summary", in Björnberg, U., *European Parents in the 1990s*, Transaction Books, 1992, p. 4.

8   Bernstam, M.S. and Swan, P.L., "Malthus and the Evolution of the Welfare State: An Essay on the Second Invisible Hand", Working Paper, 1989, 89-012, Australian Graduate School of Management, University of New South Wales.

9   *Ibid*, pp. 50-51.

10 Wilson, W.J., *The Truly Disadvantaged*, University of Chicago Press, 1987.

11 *Life at 33*, Research Briefings, No. 8, Economic and Social Research Council, 1993, p. 13.

12 Kiernan, K. and Wicks, M., *Family Change and Future Policy*, York: Joseph Rowntree Foundation in association with the Family Policy Studies Centre, 1990.

13 *Life at 33*, op. cit.

14 See Chester, R., "The Myth of the Disappearing Nuclear Family", in Anderson, D. and Dawson, G. (eds.), *Family Portraits*, London: Social Affairs Unit, 1986.

15 Kiernan, K. and Wicks, M., *op. cit.*, p. 4.

16 Hewitt, P. and Leach, P., *Social Justice, Children and Families*, London: Institute for Public Policy Research, 1993, p. 9.

17 Dench, G., *From Extended Family to State Dependency*, Centre for Community Studies, Middlesex University, 1993, p. 69; and quoting Finch, J., *Family Obligations and Social Change*, Oxford Polity Press, 1989.

18 Björnberg , U., *op. cit.*

19 Thornton, A., "Changing Attitudes Towards Family Issues in the United States", *Journal of Marriage and the Family*, Vol. 51, 1989, pp. 873-93; and Jacobs, E. and Worcester, R., *Typically British?: The Prudential Mori Guide*, Bloomsbury Press, 1990;

Reader's Digest/Mori, 1991.

20 The Farley Report, Farley Health Products Ltd, Nottingham, 1991.

21 "Britain's Teenagers", Gallup Report for the *Daily Telegraph,* 31 May 1993.

22 Wilson, W.J., in *The Truly Disadvantaged, op. cit.,* quoting work of Hogan, D.P.

23 Dennis, N. and Erdos, G., *Families without Fatherhood*, London: IEA Health and Welfare Unit, 1992, p. 70.

24 Testa, M., "Joblessness and Absent Fatherhood in the Inner City", Paper presented at the annual meeting of the American Sociological Association, 1990, p. 22, quoted in Wilson, W.J., "Research and the Truly Disadvantaged", in Jencks, C. and Peterson, P.E., *op.cit.*, p. 468.

25 Jencks, C., "Is the American Underclass Growing?", in Jencks, C. and Peterson, P.E., *op. cit.*, p. 91.

26 This view is typically expressed by one youth, whose girlfriend is pregnant:

> Maybe she thought I'd fall for her when she had a baby on the way, who knows? Either way I didn't see it as my problem. I had enough worries trying to get and keep a job and survive by myself, let alone support two other people.
>
> ... we used contraception. It failed and she didn't get it sorted out. I made it quite plain to her I was not interested in a baby at 19 and she had plenty of time to do something about it.
>
> In those laughable sex education talks at school they told us that in England a woman can have an abortion provided they get to the doctor early enough. I don't know why many girls don't bother with that and go ahead with babies ... Either way I don't see it can be the bloke's problem. If I wanted a baby, I'd have told her so and banned all Durex from the house.
>
> As it is, I feel my first responsibility is to myself. I've got to get my life sorted out, get a steady job, move out of home eventually and make a good living.

"Irresponsible Teenager", Interviews by O'Donoghue, S., *The Sunday Times*, 3 July 1994.

27 *Girl About Town*, May 1994.

28 Busfield, J. and Paddon, M., *Thinking About Children*, Cambridge, 1977.

29 Ermisch, J., *Lone Parenthood,* Cambridge University Press, 1991.

30 Deech, R., *Divorce Dissent: Dangers in Divorce Reform,* Policy Study No. 136, London: Centre for Policy Studies, 1994, p. 17.

31 Phillips, R., *Putting Asunder: A History of Divorce in Western Society,* NY: Cambridge University Press, 1988; Cherlin, A.J., *Marriage, Divorce, Remarriage,* Cambridge, Mass: Harvard University Press, 1981; and Thornton, A., "Changing Attitudes towards Separation and Divorce: Causes and Consequences", *American Journal of Sociology,* Vol. 90., No. 4, 1985, pp. 856-72; Kitson, G.C. and Morgan, L.A., "The Multiple Consequences of Divorce: A Decade Review", *Journal of Marriage and the Family,* Vol. 52, 1990, pp. 913-924.

32 Heath, A., "The Attitudes of the Underclass", in Smith, D.J. (ed.), *Understanding the Underclass,* London: Policy Studies Institute, 1992.

33 "Sex and Marriage", Mori poll for *The Times,* 28 September 1993.

34 Anderson, E., "Neighbourhood Effects on Teenage Pregnancy", in Jencks and Peterson, *op. cit.,* p. 381.

35 Anderson, E., *ibid.*

36 Ermisch, J., *op. cit.,* p. 171.

37 *Ibid.,* pp. 165-66.

38 *Ibid.,* p. 168.

39 *Ibid.,* p. 165.

40 Murray, C., *Losing Ground: American Social Policy 1950-1980,* New York: Basic Books, 1984, pp. 227-28.

41 *Ibid,* p. 227.

42 Ellwood, D.T., *Understanding Dependency,* Washington DC: US Department of Health and Human Services, 1987, p. 90.

43 Bernstam, M.S. and Swan, P.L., *op. cit.*

44 Ellwood, D.T., in *Poor Support: Poverty and the American Family,* New York: Basic Books, 1988, p. 70.

45 Duncan, G.J. and Hoffman, S.D., "Teenage Behaviour and Subsequent Pregnancy", in Jencks, C. and Peterson, P.E., *op. cit.,* p. 173.

46 Ellwood, D.T., *Poor Support ...,* *op. cit.,* p. 79.

47 Ellwood, D.T. and Summers, L.H., "Poverty in America", in Danziger, S.H. and Weinberg, D.H. (eds.), *Fighting Poverty: What Works and What Does Not,* Harvard University Press, 1986, p. 98.

48 Morgan, P., *Facing Up To Family Income,* London: National Family Trust, 1989; and Joseph, K., *The Rewards of Parenthood: Towards More Equitable Tax Treatment,* London: Centre for Policy Studies, 1990.

49 Wicks, M., *Putting Families First: A 10 Point Policy Agenda,* 1993, pp. 2 and 13.

50 McGregor, O.R., *Divorce in England*, Heinemann, 1957, p. 199.

51 Edwards, S. and Halpern, A., "Financial Provision, Case Law and Statistical Trends Since 1984", *Family Law*, Vol.17, October 1987.

52 Hoggett, B., "Ends and Means: The Utility of Marriage as a Legal Institution", in Ekalaar, J.M. and Katz, S.N. (eds.), *Marriage and Cohabitation in Contemporary Society*, Butterworth, 1980, pp. 94-103; Campion, J. and Leeson, P., "Facing Reality: the Case for the Reconstruction of Legal Marriage", *The Family Law Action Group*, 1994; Campion, J., Rein, S. and Leeson, P., "Marriage, Morals and the Law", a paper for "Empowering People in Families", 11 -15 July 1994, University of Plymouth.

53 *Facing the Future: A Discussion Paper on the Grounds for Divorce*, Law Commission No. 170, London: HMSO, 1988; and Lord Chancellor's Department, *Looking to the Future: Mediation and the Grounds for Divorce*, CM2424, London: HMSO, 1993.

54 *Looking to the Future: Mediation and the Grounds for Divorce, ibid.*

55 Hoggett, B., *op. cit.*

56 The Children Act 1989, c. 41, Pt. I and II, sections 8, 9, 10.

57 Spokeswoman for the Children's Legal Centre, quoted in the *Daily Mail*, 1 July 1994.

58 Kissman, K., *op. cit.*, p. 6.

59 Roll, J., *What is a Family: Benefit Models and Social Realities*, London: Family Policy Studies Centre, 1991, p. 76.

60 Kissman, K., *op. cit.*

61 *Families in Debt*, National Children's Home, 1992.

62 Moss, P., *Childcare and Equality of Opportunity*, Consolidated Report to the European Commission, 1988, p. 28.

63 Ward, C., Joshi, H. and Dale, A., *Income Dependency Within Couples*, National Child Development Study, Working Paper No. 36, 1993, pp. 10-11.

64 *Ibid.*, p. 18.

65 *Ibid.*, p. 11.

66 *Ibid.*, p. 5.

67 Moss, P., *op. cit.*, Consolidated Report to the European Commission, 1988, pp. 23-26.

68 Lister, R., *Women's Economic Dependency and Social Security*, Equal Opportunities Commission, 1992, p. vi.

69 Hewitt, P., Coote, A. and Harman, H., *The Family Way*, London: Institute of Public Policy Research, 1990, p. 7.

70 Foster, J., "Family Values Survey", reported in the *Daily Mail,* 9 March 1994.

71 Ward, C., Joshi, H. and Dale, A., "Income Dependency Within Couples", National Child Development Study, Working Paper, No. 36, 1993, p. 7.

72 Lister, R., *op. cit.,* p. v; Roll, J., *Lone Parents in the European Community*, London: Family Policy Studies Centre, 1992.

73 Toynbee, P., "A Woman's Work is Never Done", *The Sunday Times Review,* 14 September 1991.

74 Lister, R., *op. cit.*

75 Parker, H. (ed.), *Citizen's Income and Women*, Basic Income Research Group Discussion Paper No. 2, 1993.

76 Lister, R., *op. cit.,* p. 71.

77 *Ibid.,* p. x.

78 *Ibid.,* p. 68.

79 National Children's Home Factfile, *Children in Britain*, 1992, pp. 10-11 and 90.

80 Monk, S., *From the Margins to the Mainstream*, National Council for One Parent Families, 1993; see also Burghes, L., *One-Parent Families: Policy Options for the 1990s*, London: Family Policy Studies Centre, 1993.

81 Lister, R. *Women's Economic Dependency and Social Security*, Equal Opportunities Commission, 1992, p. 68.

82 Jordan, W., *et al., op. cit.*, pp. 305-11.

83 Day, R.D. and Mackey, W.C., "The Mother-State-Child Family: Cul de sac or Path to the Future?", *The Family in America*, Vol. 2, No. 3, March 1988, pp. 1-8; Mackey, W.C., *Fathering Behaviors*, New York: Plenum Press, 1985.

84 Bush, J., "A benefits system that does not help people to work", *The Times,* 22 July 1993.

85 Day, R.D. and Mackey, W.C., *op. cit.*, p. 4.

86 *Ibid*, p. 6.

87 Hoggett, B., *op. cit.*

88 Day, R. D. and Mackey, W.C., *op. cit.*

89 *Ibid.*

90 Dormor, D.J., *The Relationship Revolution: Cohabitation, Marriage and Divorce in Contemporary Europe*, London: One Plus One, 1992, p. 31.

Chapter 5

1   Malinowski, B., *Sex and Repression in Savage Society,* 1927, Routledge & Kegan Paul, 1960 edition, pp. 210-13.

2   Murray, D.W., "Poor Suffering Bastards: An Anthropologist Looks at Illegitimacy", *Policy Review*, No. 68, Spring 1994, pp. 9-15.

3   Toynbee, P., "What Makes a Family Happy?", *The Independent*, 17 January 1994.

4   Slipman, S., "Let's All Blame Single Mothers", *She*, March 1994.

5   Quoted in Kirk, L., "A Rothschild Takes the Helm as Norwood Approaches 200th Year", *Jewish Chronicle*, 17 June 1994.

6   Jackson, B., "Single Parent Families", in Rapoport, R.N., Fogarty, N. and Rapoport, R. (eds.), *Families in Britain*, Routledge & Kegan Paul, 1982, p. 169.

7   Poponoe, D., quoted by Whitehead, B.D., "Divorce and Kids: the Evidence is in", *Reader's Digest*, July 1994, p. 91.

8   Coote, A., Harman, H. and Hewitt, P., *The Family Way*, London: Institute for Public Policy Research, 1990, p. 27.

9   *Ibid.*, p. 29.

10 McLanahan, S., "The Consequences of Single Parenthood for Subsequent Generations", *Focus*, Wisconsin: Institute for Research on Poverty, 1988, p. 20.

11 Utting, D., Bright, J. and Henricson, C., *Crime and the Family: Improving Childrearing and Preventing Delinquency*, London: Family Policy Studies Centre, 1993, p. 20.

12 Burghes, L., *Lone Parenthood and Family Disruption*, London: Family Policy Studies Centre, 1994, p. 48.

13 Utting, D., *et al.*, *op. cit.*, p. 20.

14 Burghes, L., *op. cit.*; Toynbee, P., *op. cit.*, 17 January 1994, commenting on Crellin, E., Kellmer Pringle, M.L. and West, P., *Born Illegitimate: Social and Economic Implications*, Windsor, England: NFER, 1971; Ferri, E., *Growing Up in a One-Parent Family*, NFER, 1976.

15 Wells, L. and Rankin, J.H., "Families and Delinquency: a Meta-Analysis of the Impact of Broken Homes", *Social Problems*, Vol. 38, No. 1, 1991, pp. 71-89.

16 Hagell, A. and Newburn, T., *Persistent Young Offenders*, London: Policy Studies Institute, 1994.

17 West, D.J., *Delinquency: Its Roots, Careers and Prospects*, Heinemann, 1982.

18 Capaldi, D.M. and Patterson, G.R., "Relation of Parental Transitions to Boy's Adjustment Problems: i. A Linear Hypothesis, ii. Mothers At Risk for Transitions and Unskilled Parenting", *Developmental Psychology*, Vol. 27, No. 3, 1991, pp. 489-504.

19 Ferri, E., *Step Children*, NFER-Nelson, 1984.

20 Riley, D. and Shaw, M., *Parental Supervision and Juvenile Delinquency*, London: Home Office Research Study, No.83, 1985.

21 Coote, A., Harman, H. and Hewitt, P., *op. cit.*, p. 33.

22 See, for example, Kissman, K. and Allen, J.A., *Single Parent Families*, Sage, 1992.

23 Ferri, E., *Step Children, op. cit.*, p. 121.

24 Lempers, J.D., Lempers, D.C. and Simons, R.L., "Economic Hardship, Parenting and Distress in Adolescence", *Child Development*, Vol. 60, 1989, pp. 25-39; Takeuchi, D.T., Williams, D.R. and Adair, R.K., "Economic Stress in the Family and Children's Emotional and Behavioural Problems", *Journal of Marriage and the Family*, Vol. 53, 1991, pp. 1,031-41; Jones, L., "Unemployment and Child Abuse", *Families in Society: The Journal of Contemporary Human Services*, 1990, pp. 579-87.

25 Burghes, L., *op. cit.* pp 48-49

26 Hewitt, P. and Leach, P., *Social Justice, Children and Families*, The Commission on Social Justice, London: Institute for Public Policy Research, 1993, p. 8.

27 Crellin, E., Pringle, M.L.K. and West, P., *Born Illegitimate*, report for the National Children's Bureau, National Foundation for Educational Research, 1971; Eberstadt, M., "Is Illegitimacy a Public Health Hazard?", *National Review*, 30 December 1988.

28 Manderbacka, K. *et al.*, "Marital Status as a Predictor of Perinatal Outcome in Finland", *Journal of Marriage and the Family*, Vol. 54, 1992, pp. 508-15.

29 Wright, R.E., *Sexual Union Status and Infant Mortality in Jamaica*, unpublished manuscript, Department of Political Economy, University of Glasgow, 1994.

30 Dubow, E.F. and Luster, T., "Adjustment of Children Born to Teenage Mothers: The Contribution of Risk and Protective Factors", *Journal of Marriage and the Family*, Vol. 52, 1990, pp. 393-404; Lummis, T., "The Historical Dimension of Fatherhood: A Case Study 1890-1914", in McKee, L. and O'Brian, M., *The Father Figure*, Tavistock, 1982.

31 Judge, K. and Benzeval, M., "Health Inequalities: New Concerns about the children of single mothers", *British Medical Journal*, Vol. 306, 13 March 1993.

32 See papers in Lamb, M.E. (ed.), *The Role of the Father in Child Development*, Wiley, 1981; Cox, M.J., *et al.*, "Marriage, Adult Adjustment, and Early Parenting", *Child Development*, Vol. 60, 1989, pp. 1,015-24.

33 Murray, D.W., *op. cit.*, p. 10.

34 "Children Living in Re-ordered Families", *Social Policy Research Findings,* No. 45, York: Joseph Rowntree Foundation, February 1994.

35 Dominian, J., *et al.*, *Marital Breakdown and the Health of the Nation*, London: One Plus One, 1991; McLanahan, S. and Booth, K., "Mother-Only Families: Problems, Prospects and Politics", *Journal of Marriage and the Family*, Vol. 51, 1989, p. 557.

36 Gartner, R., "Family Structure, Welfare Spending, and Child Homicide in Developed Democracies", *Journal of Marriage and The Family*, 1991, Vol. 53, pp. 231-240.

37 Creighton, S.J., and Noyes, P., *Child Abuse Trends in England and Wales 1983-87,* London: National Society for the Prevention of Cruelty to Children, 1989.

38 Rutter, M. and Quinton, D., "Long-term Follow-up of Women Institutionalised in Childhood: Factors Promoting Good Functioning in Adult Life", *British Journal of Developmental Psychology*, Vol. 2, 1984, pp. 191-204.

39 Gordon, M. and Creighton, S.J. "Natal and Non-Natal Fathers as Sexual Abusers in the United Kingdom: A Comparative Analysis", *Journal of Marriage and the Family*, Vol. 50, 1988, pp. 99-105.

40 Whelan, R., *Broken Homes and Battered Children*, Oxford: Family Education Trust, 1994.

41 Daly, M., and Wilson, M., "Body and Mind: Darwinism and the Human Sciences", *LSE Magazine*, Autumn 1993, pp. 22-24, reprinted from the *Times Higher Educational Supplement*, 25 June 1993.

42 *Ibid.*

43 Ferri, E., *Step Children, op. cit.*

44 Gartner, R., *op. cit.,*

45 Burdekin Report: Report of the National Inquiry into Homeless Children, *Our Homeless Children*, Canberra: AGPS, 1989, discussed in Tapper, A., *The Family in the Welfare State*, Allen & Unwin and the Australian Institute for Public Policy, p. 202.

46 Kiernan, K., "The Impact of Family Disruption in Childhood on Transitions Made in Young Adult Life", *Population Studies*, Vol. 46, 1992, pp. 213-34.

47 See "Aspirations for Adolescent Services and Housing under the Children Act", in McCluskey, J., *Reassessing Priorities: The Children Act 1989–A New Agenda for Young Homeless People*, CHAR, Housing Campaign for Single People, 1993.

48 *National Prison Survey Research Study*, No. 128, Home Office, Research and Statistics Department, 1991.

49 Essen, J., Lambert, L. and Head, J., "School Attainment of Children Who Have Been in Care", *Child: Care, Health and Development*, Vol. 2, No. 6, 1976, pp. 339-51.

50 Bebbington, A. and Miles, J., "The Background of Children who Enter Local Authority Care", *British Journal of Social Work*, Vol. 19, 1989, pp. 349-68.

51 Marsh, P., "Social Work and Fathers—An Exclusive Practice?", in Lewis, C. and O'Brien, M., *Reassessing Fatherhood*, Sage, 1987.

52 For example, Utting, D., Bright, J. and Henricson, C., *Crime and the Family: Improving Child-Rearing and Preventing Delinquency*, London: Family Policy Studies Centre, 1993.

53 McLanahan, S. and Booth, K., "Mother-Only Families: Problems, Prospects, and Politics", *Journal of Marriage and the Family*, Vol. 51, 1989, pp. 557-80; McLanahan, S., "The Consequences of Single Parenthood for Subsequent Generations", *Focus*, Institute for Research on Poverty, University of Winsconsin-Madison, 1988, p. 21.

54 Dominian, J. *et al., Marital Breakdown and the Health of the Nation, op. cit.,* p. 4.

55 McLanahan, S. and Booth, K., *op. cit.,* p. 564, referring primarily to Herzog, E. and Sudia, C.E., *Boys in Fatherless Families*, Washington DC: US Department of Health, Education and Welfare, 1970.

56 *Ibid.,* p. 565.

57 Burghes, L., *op. cit.,* p. 15.

58 McLanahan, S., "The Reproduction of Poverty", *American Journal of Sociology,* Vol. 90, 1985, pp. 873-901.

59 McLanahan, S. and Booth, K., *op. cit.*

60 McLanahan, S., "Family Structure and Dependency: Early Transitions to Female Household Headship", *Demography*, Vol. 25, No. 1, 1988, pp. 1-15.

61 Aquilino, W.S., "Family Structure and Home Leaving: A Further Specification of the Relationship", *Journal of Marriage and the Family*, No. 53, 1991, pp. 999-1,010.

62 Dornbusch, S.M. *et al.,* "Single Parents, Extended Households, and the Control of Adolescents", *Child Development,* Vol. 56, 1985, pp. 326-41.

63 Krein, S.F. and Beller, A.H., "Educational Attainment of Children from Single-Parent Families: Differences by Exposure, Gender and Race", *Demography*, Vol. 25, No. 2, 1988, pp. 221-33.

64 Kellam, S. *et al*, "The Long-term Evolution of the Family Structure of Teenage and Older Mothers", *Journal of Marriage and the Family*, Vol. 44, 1982, pp.539-54.

65 Dawson, D.A., *Family Structure and Children's Health: United States 1988*, Series 10:178 Vital and Health Statistics, Maryland: US Department of Health and Human Services, 1991; Pilling, D., *Escape from Disadvantage*, London: The Falmer Press, 1990.

66 Osborn, A.F., Butler, N.R. and Morris, A.C., *The Social Life of Britain's Five Year Olds*, Routledge & Kegan Paul, 1984.

67 McLanahan, S., *op. cit.*, "The Consequences for Single Parenthood For Subsequent Generations".

68 Steinberg, L., "Single Parents, Stepparents, and the Susceptibility of Adolescents to Antisocial Peer Pressure", *Child Development*, Vol. 58, 1987, pp. 269-75.

69 Scarr, S. *et al.*, "Developmental Status and School Achievements of Minority and Non-Minority Children from Birth to 18 Years in a British Midlands Town", *British Journal of Development Psychology*, No. 1, 1983, pp. 31-48.

70 Newson, E., Newson, J. and Lewis, C., "Father Participation Through Childhood and its Relationship with Career Aspirations and Delinquency", in Beail, N. and McGuire, J. (eds.), *Fathers: Psychological Perspectives*, Junction Books, 1982.

71   Lambert, L. and Hart, S., "Who Needs a Father?", *New Society*, Vol. 37, No. 718, 1976, p. 80.

72 Crellin, E. *et al.*, *op. cit.*; Ferri, E., *Growing Up in a One-Parent Family: a Long-term Study of Child Development*, Slough: NFER, 1976; Essen, J., "Living in One-Parent Families: Attainment at School", *Child: Care, Health and Development*, Vol. 5, 1979, pp. 189-200; Burghes, L., *op. cit.*; quotes in text are from summary in Fogelman, K. (ed.), *Growing Up in Great Britain*, Macmillan for the National Children's Bureau, 1983, pp. 101-08.

73 Whitehead, B.D., "Dan Quayle was Right", *The Atlantic Monthly*, April, 1993, p. 80.

74 Coote, A., *et al., op. cit.*, p. 31.

75 Utting, D., *et al., op. cit.*, p. 22.

76 Wadsworth, M., *The Roots of Delinquency*, Martin Robertson, 1979, see p. 115.

77 West, D.J. and Farrington, D.P., *Who Becomes Delinquent?*, Heinemann, 1973; and *The Delinquent Way of Life,* Heinemann, 1977.

78 McCord, J., "A Longitudinal View of the Relationship between Paternal Absence and Crime", in Gunn, J. and Farrington, D.P. (eds.), *Abnormal Offenders, Delinquency, and the Criminal Justice System*, John Wiley & Sons, 1982.

79 *Ibid.*, p. 125.

80 Offord, D.R., "Family Backgrounds of Male and Female Delinquents", in Gunn, J. and Farrington, D.P., *op. cit.*, pp. 129-51.

81 Dawson, D.A., *op. cit.*

82 Dornbusch, S.M. *et al.*, *op. cit.*, p. 340.

83 McLanahan, S., "The Consequences of Single Parenthood for Subsequent Generations", *op. cit.*, p. 20.

84 Wallerstein, J.S., and Blakeslee, S., *Second Chances*, Ticknor and Fields, 1989, p. 234.

85 *Social Policy Research Findings*, No. 45, York: Joseph Rowntree Foundation, February 1994.

86 Coote, A., *et al.*, *op. cit.*

87 Wallerstein, J.S. and Blakeslee, S., *op. cit.*, pp. 52-53.

88 Ermisch, J., "Familia Oeconomica: A Survey of the Economics of the Family", *Scottish Journal of Political Economy*, Vol. 40, No. 4, 1993, pp. 353-74.

89 Matsueda, R.L. and Heimer, K., "Race, Family Structure, and Delinquency: A Test of Differential Association and Social Control Theories", *American Sociological Review*, Vol. 52, 1987, pp. 826-40.

90 Haskins, R., "Beyond Metaphor: The Efficacy of Early Childhood Education", *American Psychologist*, February 1989, pp. 274-81; Berrueta-Clement, J.R. *et al.*, *Changed Lives: The Effects of the Perry Pre-School Program on Youths Through Age 19*, MI: High/Scope, 1985; Osborn, A.F. and Milbank, J.E., *The Effects of Early Education*, Clarendon Press, 1987.

91 Haskins, R., *op. cit.*, p. 279.

92 Utting, D., *et al.*, *op. cit.*, p. 57, in reference to Graham, J. and Smith, D.I., *Diversion from Offending: The Role of the Youth Service*, Crime Concern, 1993.

93 Sampson, R. J., "Crime in Cities: The Effects of Formal and Informal Social Control", in Reiss, Jnr., A.J. and Tony, M. (eds.), *Communities and Crime*, Vol. 8 in *Crime and Justice*, University of Chicago Press, 1987.

94 Sampson, R.J., "Does an Intact Family reduce Burglary Risks for Neighbours?", *Sociology and Social Research*, Vol. 71, 1987, pp. 404-07.

95 Smith, D. and Jarjoura, G.R., "Social Structure and Criminal Victimisation", *Journal of Research in Crime and Delinquency*, Vol. 25, February 1988, pp. 27-52.

96 Hill, M.A. and O'Neill, J., *Underclass Behaviors in the United States: Measurement and Analysis of Determinants*, City University of New York, Baruch College, 1993.

97 Sampson, R.J., "Urban Black Violence: The Effect of Male Joblessness and Family Disruption", *American Journal of Sociology*, Vol. 93, No. 2, 1987, pp. 348-82.

98 Murray, D.W., *op. cit.*, p. 13.

99 Suttles, G., *The Social Order of the Slum*, University of Chicago Press, 1968; and *The Social Construction of Communities*, University of Chicago Press, 1972.

100 Dench, G., *From Extended Family to State Dependency*, Centre for Community Studies, Middlesex University, 1993, p. 7.

101 *Ibid.*, p. 61.

102 Tapper, A., *The Family in the Welfare State*, Allen & Unwin and the Australian Institute for Public Policy, 1990, p. 207.

103 Dominian, J. *et al.*, *Marital Breakdown and the Health of the Nation*, London: One Plus One, 1991, pp. 13, 16-17.

104 Field, S. and Southgate, P., *Public Disorder: A Review of Research and a Study in one Inner City Area*, London: HMSO, Study No. 72, 1982; Moens, F.G.G. *et al.*, "Epidemiological Aspects of Suicide Among the Young in Selected European Countries", *Journal of Epidemiology and Community Health*, Vol. 42, 1988, pp. 431-47.

105 Sampson, R.J., "Urban Black Violence ...", *op. cit.*

106 Sampson, R.J., "Does an Intact Family Reduce Burglary Risks for Its Neighbours?", *Sociology and Social Research,* Vol. 71, 1987, pp. 404-07.

107 Breault, K.D., "Suicide in America: The Test of Durkheim's Theory of Religious and Family Integration, 1933-1980", *American Journal of Sociology*, Vol. 92, 1986, pp. 651-52.

108 Stack, S., "The Impact of Divorce on Suicide in Norway, 1951-1980", *Journal of Marriage and the Family*, Vol. 51, 1989, pp. 229-38; "The Effect of Suicide in Denmark, 1961-1980", *The Sociological Quarterly*, Vol. 31, 1990, pp. 361-68.

109 Matza, D., *Delinquency and Drift*, Chichester: John Wiley & Sons, 1964, p. 55.

110 Murray, D.W., *op. cit.,* p. 9.

111 Will, G.F., "Nature and the Male Sex", *Newsweek*, 7 June 1991.

112 Utting, D. *et al., op. cit.;* and also see Coote, A. (ed.), *Families, Children and Crime*, London: Institute for Public Policy Research, 1994.

113 Snarey, J. *et al.*, "The Role of Parenting in Men's Psychosocial Development: A Longitudinal Study of Early Adulthood Infertility and Midlife Generativity", *Developmental Psychology*, Vol. 23, No. 4, 1987, pp. 593-603; and Sundeen, R.A., "Family Life Course Status and Volunteer Behaviour", *Sociological Perspectives*, Vol. 33, No. 4, 1990, pp. 483-500.

114 Gilder, G., *Sexual Suicide*, New York: Quadrangle, 1973, p. 99, quoted in Dench, G., *op. cit.*, p. 53.

115 Dench, G., *op. cit.*, p. 74.

116 Carlson, A.C., "What Happened to the Family Wage?", *The Public Interest,* Spring 1986, p. 4.

117 Malthus, T., *Essay on Population*, originally published 1798, Everyman edition, p. 161.

118 Gilder, G., *Wealth and Poverty*, London: Buchan and Enright, 1982, p. 76.

119 *Ibid.*, p. 9.

120 Greer, G., *Sex and Destiny*, London: Secker and Warburg, 1984, p. 47.

121 Simms, M. and Smith, C., "Young Fathers: Attitudes to Marriage and Family Life", in McKee, L. and O'Brien, M. (eds.), *The Father Figure*, Tavistock, 1982, pp. 147-48.

122 See discussion in Christiansen, G.B. and Williams, W.R., "Welfare, Family Cohesiveness and Out of Wedlock Births", in Peden, J.R. and Glahe, F.R. (eds.), *The American Family and the State*, San Francisco: Pacific Research Institute, 1986; Garfinkel, I. and Haveman, R., *Earnings Capacity and Inequality*, New York: Academic Press, 1977.

123 Ferri, E., *Life at 33, op. cit.*

124 Wilkie, J.R., "The Decline in Men's Labor Force Participation and Income and the Changing Structure of Family Economic Support", *Journal of Marriage and the Family*, No. 53, 1991, pp. 111-22.

125 Mansfield, P. and Collard, J., *The Beginning of the Rest of Your Life*, Macmillan, 1988, pp. 51-52.

126 *Ibid.*, pp. 141-42.

127 Dench, G., *op. cit.*, p. 9.

128 Hutton, W., "Why Women Must Be Central to the Left", *The Guardian*, 18 April 1994.

129 Bernstein, M.S. and Swan, P.L., "Malthus and the Evolution of the Welfare State: An Essay on the Second Invisible Hand", Working Paper 89-012, University of New South Wales, Australian Graduate School of Management, 1989.

Conclusion

1 Day, R.D. and Mackey, W.C., "The Mother-State-Child 'Family': Cul-de-Sac or Path to the Future?", *The Family in America*, Vol. 2, No. 3, Rockford Institute, March 1988.

2 Levy, M., *Feminism and Freedom*, Transaction, 1987, p. 284.

3 Engels, F., *The Origins of the Family, Private Property and the State* (first published 1884), London: Granada Publishing, 1972.

4 Berger, P. and B., *The War over the Family*, London: Hutchinson, 1983, pp. 192-93.

5 Malinowski, B., *Sex and Repression in Savage Society,* (first published 1927), London: Routledge, 1960, p. 212; see also Delaney, C., "The Meaning of Paternity and the Virgin Birth Debate", *Man,* Vol. 21, No. 3, 1986; and Fortes, M., "Rules and the Emergence of Human Society", Royal Anthropological Institute, Occasional Paper No. 39, 1983.

6 Murray, D.W., "Poor Suffering Bastards: An Anthropologist Looks at Illegitimacy", *Policy Review*, No. 68, Spring 1994, p. 9; and Wilson, W.J. and Neckerman, K.M., "Poverty and Family Structure", in Danziger, S.H. and Weinberg, D.H., *Fighting Poverty: What Works and What Does Not*, Cambridge, Mass: Harvard University Press, 1986, p. 259.

7 Scott, J., Braun, M. and Alwin, D., "The Family Way" in Jowell, R. *et al., International Social Attitudes: The 10th BSA Report*, Dartmouth Publishing Company, 1993, pp. 42 and 45.

8 Leonard, T., "New Survey Kills Dream of the Perfect Family", *Evening Standard*, 25 January 1994.